National Bestseller

Named a Best Book of the Year by *Quill & Quire*
and the *Globe and Mail*

Winner of the Rakuten Kobo
Emerging Writer Prize for Nonfiction

Nominated for the Evergreen Award

"An essential read." —*Globe and Mail*

"I wish I had been able to read Eternity Martis when I was an undergraduate. Astute, witty, and fiercely honest, *They Said This Would Be Fun* is required reading for anyone yearning for better institutions and relations of learning." —David Chariandy, Governor General's Literary Award–winning author of *Brother* and *I've Been Meaning to Tell You*

"A landmark among memoirs. . . . Martis, whose writing flows smoothly and deceptively calmly, has written a meticulous unravelling of her coming of age." —*Toronto Star*

"When I read this book I felt seen. The year I spent at Western University was one of my loneliest. I'd never felt so Black and female in my life. While Eternity's study of campus life for Black women is groundbreaking it is not at all foreign to Black students who seek higher education. It's a must read for every post-secondary student and educator." —Tracy Moore, host of *Cityline*

"I'm a twenty-something person in a world that believes twenty-something-year-olds can't face, let alone overcome, deep challenges. Then I read Eternity Martis's book and I felt seen, if perhaps for the first time. *They Said This Would Be Fun* offers validation, no matter your own personal circumstances, with just the right amount of humour, suspense, and theory. It's a call to action, a manual for allies, an unapologetic truth for people like us. Focusing on Martis's experience as a Black woman in a predominantly white university, this book makes tangible the daily, overt, and normalized racism so well stitched in our institutions. It celebrates friendship and closely evaluates intimate partner violence. . . . Beyond being heart-shattering and thought-provoking, there's this brilliant and intentional prose that shapeshifts per chapter, and this is what makes it fun: part memoir, part survivor guide. . . . This book will pull you in, make you laugh, eat you up and leave you better than you were before." —Téa Mutonji, 2020 Trillium Book Award–winning author of *Shut Up You're Pretty*

"The humour and introspection with which Martis writes about her difficult experiences make her first book a multi-dimensional read." —*Quill & Quire*

"[Martis] is so generous in her storytelling, so gifted in the way she sorts through her feelings, and her honesty is awe-inspiring. Her essays . . . stick with you for days after finishing them. . . . I can't say enough about the magnitude of this book, of the way it feels like she's sitting next to you, simply sharing her story." —Anne T. Donahue, author of *Nobody Cares: Essays*

"A testament to the transformative power of Black feminism." —*The Star*

"To say *They Said This Would Be Fun* is a timely read would do a disservice to its staying power. It's a book that should be required reading now and in the years to come. Fiercely honest, meticulously researched, and deeply personal, it is an excellent account of what it means to be a Black woman in a Canadian university—and a Black woman in Canada." —*Literary Review of Canada*

"[Martis] breaks down her university experiences with tact and humour, weaving together the complicated dynamics of race with themes of self-discovery, systems of oppression, and relationships—all under an overarching feminist frame." —*Varsity*

"Martis writes boldly about her experience in this unique memoir that testifies how a support group of women of colour can change someone's personal narrative." —*NOW Magazine*

"Anyone working in postsecondary education should read [Martis's] memoir. You'll get a better, and sobering, understanding of what Black and Indigenous students experience day-in and day-out both on-campus and in the community." —Jay Robb, *Leaders are Readers*

"I'm angry to hear that Canadian universities are still ignoring and isolating young racialized women, decades after my own experiences there. But I'm very glad that [Martis's] brave, honest, and funny book will be there for students of the future—as well as for institutions whose leaders have the courage and decency to change." —Denise Balkissoon, Executive Editor, *Chatelaine*

"With fierce intelligence and flashes of humour, Eternity Martis exposes racism and sexism on contemporary university campuses through her personal story of coming of age as a young Black woman at a predominantly white school. A deeply felt memoir about resistance, resilience, and the life-saving power of finding your own voice." —Rachel Giese, author of *Boys: What It Means to Become a Man*

"[Martis's] writing is both candid and alluring and perfectly delineates how race, gender, and sexuality are all intertwined in everyday events of university life. This book is an urgent read for all educators and education administrators, those who are considering university and college life in Canada, alongside young Black and racialized women who are looking to be seen." —Huda Hassan, writer and researcher

"Though *They Said This Would Be Fun* is Eternity Martis's debut, she is an authority on the pervasive nature of racism on North American university campuses—an oft-overlooked issue kept hush among so-called polite Canadians. *They Said This Would Be Fun* is not an easy read, nor is it always comfortable. But it is an essential book for allies—an exhaustive look at the discrimination Black women face in a country too often described as a haven of multiculturalism." —Erica Lenti, Senior Editor, *Xtra*

"With this spellbinding and important memoir . . . Martis offers us a clear-eyed, eloquent, and no holds-barred portrayal of what it's like to be a young Black woman studying in the 'ivory tower'. . . . Unwaveringly unapologetic, richly written, and powerfully conveyed, Martis offers us the book that scholars, students, and university administrators have been waiting for—an unflinching look at racism on Canadian campuses. Following in the footsteps of writers like Roxane Gay and Scaachi Koul, but steadfastly providing her own distinctive voice, Martis's book is at times shocking, powerful, surprisingly funny, and most of all provides a seamless link between theoretical approaches to race and how it plays out in practice." —Minelle Mahtani, Associate Professor, Department of Gender, Race, Sexuality and Social Justice, and Senior Advisor to the Provost on Racialized Faculty, University of British Columbia

"University is a time of major personal growth and excitement but also systemic, baked-in discrimination and inequity. This book is for anyone who is still making sense of it all but especially for those who need communion with a beautifully-written account of what it's like to finally find your people." —Hannah Sung, journalist

THEY SAID THIS WOULD BE FUN

ETERNITY MARTIS

Race, Campus Life, and Growing Up

McClelland & Stewart

This paperback edition published 2021
Hardcover edition published 2020

McClelland & Stewart and colophon are registered trademarks of
Penguin Random House Canada Limited.

LIBRARY AND ARCHIVES CANADA CATALOGUING IN PUBLICATION
Title: They said this would be fun : race, campus life, and growing up / Eternity Martis.
Names: Martis, Eternity, author.
Identifiers: Canadiana 20190162511 | ISBN 9780771062209 (softcover)
Subjects: LCSH: Martis, Eternity. | LCSH: Martis, Eternity—Childhood and youth. |
LCSH: Discrimination in higher education—Canada. | LCSH: Blacks—Education
(Higher)—Canada. | LCSH: Women, Black—Education (Higher)—Canada. | LCSH:
Students, Black—Canada. | LCSH: Students, Black—Canada—Social conditions. |
LCSH: Minorities—Education (Higher)—Canada.
Classification: LCC LC212.43.C2 M37 2021 | DDC 371.829/96071—dc23

Cover design by Talia Abramson

Printed in the United States of America

McClelland & Stewart,
a division of Penguin Random House Canada Limited,
a Penguin Random House Company

www.penguinrandomhouse.ca

3 4 5   25 24 23

Penguin
Random House
McCLELLAND & STEWART

For M and D, for everything.

"If you are silent about your pain,
they'll kill you and say you enjoyed it."

—ZORA NEALE HURSTON

contents

introduction

As I launched out the window of an inflatable bouncy castle, into the warm autumn air and then the mud below, the only thought undiluted by copious amounts of alcohol was: *This is what freedom feels like.*

It was Saturday, the last night of Orientation Week, and hundreds of first-years were coming together to celebrate on University College Hill, a giant grassy quad on campus. Western University was known for having the most epic frosh week in Canada, especially on the last night, when a B-list Canadian band always played. This year, it was Down With Webster. Sex with Sue, the infamous old lady who we watched after-hours on TV while our parents slept, would show us how to put on condoms, and loud music would play all night alongside carnival games, corporate sponsors and their free grub, and bouncy castles.

A week ago, I had been sobbing in the basement of the house where I grew up, clutching my high school boyfriend's tear- and snot-stained shirt and cursing myself for thinking I could handle moving away from home. I cried the whole way to London, past the small cities I had never heard of and the luscious Green Belt. I cried as I walked up to my new room in Medway-Sydenham Hall and looked at the small space, crammed with two twin beds and two desks, that my best friend Taz and I would be sharing. I cried as I unpacked boxes, as I put my mattress protector on, as I wiped down empty drawers, as I unloaded my underwear from the vacuum-sealed bag and folded them neatly. I cried as I closed the drawer. I cried when I realized there were no other brown-skinned girls on our floor besides us. I cried so much that my floormates and their parents were calling me "the crying girl."

The welcome package had given us tips on how to pack, but it didn't specify how much we needed to bring. My family didn't know either—I was the first and only one to go to a Canadian university—so I brought every bra I owned, every spare sock, pair of shoes, and picture frame from my bedroom. It took twice as many sophs, the volunteer students who help first-years adjust to student life, to haul my stuff up to the third floor and make it fit into the shared fifteen-by-twelve-foot space. At one point, they lost the bag full of my pants and I was inconsolable, thinking that I'd have to walk around pantless because nobody would sell fashionable bottoms in a place nicknamed "Forest City."

When I had told people back home that I was going to Western in the fall, they had similar comments: *It's the best school. It's a party school. It's a white school—why would you go there?* Their eyes widened and they'd lean in, whispering as if they were afraid of someone hearing, and say that London was notoriously white, Christian, and conservative. They told me cautionary tales of family and friends transferring out of the school after years of microaggressions and racial harassment on and off campus. "Don't worry though," they'd say with a smile. "You'll have fun."

It had never occurred to me that other cities in Ontario wouldn't be as welcoming as the one where I'd grown up. In Toronto, there was always a mix of various ethnicities—Chinese, German, Filipino, Trinidadian, Somali, Indian, Pakistani, Sri Lankan, Jamaican, Guyanese. You can find numerous types of cuisine, schools, and places of worship on any given block. All around, people look like you and look unlike you and it's nothing to fuss about.

But listening to people's concerns, it was like I had chosen the Alabama of Canada to spend the next few years of my life in. It wasn't that my hometown was exempt from racism—I knew which department stores would send their white employees following after me like a criminal, and I understood the intentions of the police when my peers would get stopped on their way home from playing basketball. But I was sheltered; I hadn't gotten a complete picture of what it meant to be a Black girl at home before I left to become a Black woman in London. I wondered if I could form my own identity surrounded by white kids wearing Hunter boots and Canada Goose jackets. I worried I could be alienated for being "too Black." I was even more worried about losing myself and being called "too white" when I got back home.

But people in London were friendly. They smiled as you passed by. Strangers said good morning. Everyone talked to me—the women in line at the grocery store; the people sitting next to me at a restaurant; the students also waiting an unacceptably long time for the bus. But many of our conversations ended up diverting into race. *We don't get a lot of Black people here. London has become very progressive in the last few years. My God, Black people are just so funny. Where are you from? No, no no, like where did you originally come from? Ethiopia? Kenya? Zimbabwe? Africa?* As the months and years went on, these seemingly innocuous comments became more ignorant, and at times, malicious.

From the ages of eighteen to twenty-two, I learned more about what someone like me brought out in other people than about who I was. I didn't even get a chance to know myself before I had to fight for myself.

In the four years I spent in London, Ontario, for my undergraduate degree, I was called Ebony, Dark Chocolate, Shaniqua, Ma, and Boo. I encountered blackface on Halloween and was told to go back to my country on several occasions. I was humiliated by guys shouting, "Look at that black ass!" as I walked down a busy street. I was an ethnic conquest for curious white men, and the token Black friend for white women. I was called a Black bitch and a nigger. I was asked by white friends desperately trying to rap every song off *Yeezus* if it was okay to use nigga around me. I was verbally assaulted and came close to being physically attacked by angry men. I came face-to-face with a white supremacist. I was asked if I spoke English and whether I was adjusting to Canadian winters. When I told people I was born in Canada, they'd impatiently badger me with, "But where are you *really* from?"

These encounters were about how I was perceived, not who I actually was—someone always in between worlds: a Canadian-born girl with two immigrant parents; a multiracial woman with Black features in a family of brown people; a daughter raised by a working-class mother and middle-class grandparents; the only baby born out of wedlock in a family all conceived after marriage; an only child with at least seven half-siblings; an astrology-lover born right on the cusp of Taurus and Gemini.

I have lived in the squishy middle all my life, at the margins of binaries—an experience that has made me as independent as I am lonely.

I felt trapped by these categories, whose walls felt so high that I might never get out. I wondered what kind of person I was outside those confines, and university seemed like a good place to start solidifying the pieces of myself that I felt I couldn't explore back home.

A few things did solidify about my identity while I was there: I was Black, I was a woman, and I was out of place. I didn't identify as Black until I got to London. This is common among people who come to Canada from countries with diverse ethnic communities, or who grew up in a mixed family where identity wasn't discussed. I wasn't ignorant to my own appearance; I definitely didn't pass as white, and there was no way I looked brown. At home, being a racial minority meant you belonged somewhere. In London, it was a marker of exclusion and difference, and you were squeezed into a category—Black, White, Asian, Brown—that became a way to navigate and survive the environment.

My maternal grandparents, who raised me for the first half of my life, faced racism themselves when they arrived in Toronto from Karachi, Pakistan, in the early 1970s. But they didn't know what to make of my claims of anti-Black racism. We never spoke about my father, a Jamaican man, who was absent, or what his ethnicity meant for my own identity. My family was shocked to hear me call myself Black, and even more shocked at the stories I told, despite police-reported hate crimes across the country soaring the year before I went to Western, and London having one of the highest rates of all Ontario metropolises. It was 2010, and we were only starting to get to a place where advocacy journalism and personal essays extensively covered these problems. Modern Black writers like Ta-Nehisi Coates, Roxane Gay, Kiese Laymon, Morgan Jerkins, Reni Eddo-Lodge, and Ijeoma Oluo had yet to get the recognition they deserved—or even to write their stories. I had few examples to prove racism was a common occurrence and not an isolated experience.

My family thought that perhaps I was exaggerating. That I had developed a new, somewhat militant eye for race issues. Plus, I was so *angry* these days—maybe my irritability, they gently offered, was causing me to misunderstand people's intentions.

Of course I was angry. Instead of focusing on classes and adjusting to my new life as a student, everything had become about the skin I was in. I became a survivor of both intimate partner violence and sexual assault, and had to fight stereotypes about not being the perfect victim. Anger and fear were so etched in my body that I often felt I had no control over myself. Why could people take their anger out on me, but mine was irrational?

I internalized people's doubts about my experiences. I grew stressed, anxious, and depressed, coping with food, alcohol, and partying. In public, I devised exit plans in case I was harassed. Everywhere I went, even in my own home, I felt a constant, electrifying pressure in the air, as if violence could erupt at any moment.

I kept a record of all the instances where I had been the target of discrimination, harassment, and microaggressions, scribbling them down on pieces of paper—notes to myself, a way to make sense of what was happening. At school, I naturally gravitated towards students of colour who were having similar experiences. Some couldn't make it, even with our support system, and they dropped out or transferred schools. I decided to stay, weighing up the discomforts of starting over someplace new and the discomfort I was already familiar with. I accepted the emotional cost of this decision.

The year after I graduated from Western, I wrote a reported personal essay for Vice Canada, titled "London, Ontario, Was a Racist Asshole to Me." I interviewed current students, city councillors and locals. The essay sparked heated discussions in homes, in city council, and in universities, and is still a point of reference for media when discussing race-related issues such as carding, the illegal police procedure of randomly stopping people of colour and collecting information.

I received hundreds of messages from people who read the article. Londoners promised to be better allies. People who had witnessed the racial harassment of friends asked for advice on how to intervene. Older folks recalled their experiences from decades ago, saying things hadn't changed. People of colour of all ages and backgrounds shared their own stories.

Londoners confessed secrets about the tricks their bosses used to keep Black people out of their establishments. Women and LGBTQ2S+ people told me about their own horrible experiences, from verbal slurs to physical assault, especially in nightclubs. Former residents of London told me they'd left because the racism was so bad. Current inhabitants told me that they were afraid for their lives.

Most of all, students attending other post-secondary schools in Canada shared their experiences and concerns, many of which mirrored my own. And high school students messaged me, worried about which colleges and universities were racially tolerant. In the years following the article's publication, I've met students of colour around the world who've told me stories of the racism and isolation they experienced while attending university in the U.K., Australia, and the U.S.

To be clear, this isn't just a Western University problem. Here in Canada, we have nearly one hundred universities and even more colleges, and yet there's no evidence that we collect race-based data on students, so it's impossible to know how many are visible minorities and what their needs and challenges are. There is also no unified, formal policy across schools on dealing with racism. Many students don't report incidents because they fear they won't be believed.

When our experiences are treated like they don't matter, we learn to deal with them ourselves, especially when the institutions where we spend the first years of adulthood aren't equipped to support us. But young people in post-secondary institutions today are up against a host of serious, life-changing issues.

In Canada, university-age young women face the highest rates of sexual assault and intimate partner violence in the country, and are stalked, cyberstalked, and harassed more than any other age group. Carding disproportionately affects young Black and Indigenous men. Young people living with a shaky socio-economic status are pressured to get a degree, and both have been linked to an increase in mental health issues. Racism and discrimination have devastating physical and mental health effects on students, which is linked to poor academic performance and dropout rates. And we are experiencing all of this while navigating the school system. Before our brains have even finished developing. Before we even get to know who we are.

So yes, our experiences matter. This shit is actually happening right now to our young people.

On top of all that, students of colour are living and studying during a time when the far right is using universities to its own advantage. Endless stories have made the news: white pride groups putting out pro-white flyers on campuses; white nationalists using university spaces to spew anti-immigration, anti-LGBTQ2S+, anti-woman hate under the guise of free speech; hate groups trying to convert young, angry men into joining their cause. All this coverage highlights white supremacy, not the students living under it.

We promise students that university will be the time of their lives, that they will come to know themselves, that it will be *fun*. But for many of us, the whole university experience—the independence, parties, exploration, sex, wild nights—may not be possible. Not when we may deal with racism, sexism, homophobia, transphobia, and assault—physical and sexual—from our peers and the people around us. This perceived utopia can also be unbearable and unsafe.

I wrote this book to bring attention to what is happening inside our schools. For years, I've collected these moments, trying to find the right format—a play, a blog, a novel—but nothing seemed more fitting than a memoir. I've used my own experiences, as well as examples from across Canadian universities, to illustrate that this is a nationwide issue that demands attention.

Thanks to the generosity and selflessness of my grandfather, I've had the privilege of going to university, an opportunity and luxury I know many do not have. I hope to put this privilege to good use here, by illuminating the not-so-secret lives of university students: the messy, complicated, exciting but harrowing experience of what it's like to be a student and woman of colour today.

Nothing in this book is sugar-coated for you. It's raw. It's glaring. It's imperfect, as is real life. I did not make all the right decisions, or all the smart ones, and I've made peace with that. I have done my absolute best to recall everything as accurately as I can. At times, this book is distressing, and at other times you will laugh. Some events may bring back painful memories of your own.

I have chosen not to hold back because, for so long, young people have been infantilized and shamed for talking about the things that affect us. We're told we haven't worked long enough, lived long enough, been through enough to have our own pain validated. I hope this book will be an urgent reminder that dismissing the experiences of young people today will have serious, permanent implications for our entire society.

Finally, this book is for anyone, past or present, who has struggled to make sense of their post-secondary experiences.

For those of you who feel alone and unheard. For those of you who want to learn more, and for those of you who courageously speak up and tell your stories, even in the face of denial and harassment. And this book is especially for those of you who came out at the other end, broken but not beat, resilient but still soft.

I see you.

all
i
wanted
was
to
be
wonder
woman

The first time I ever held a bong, I deep-throated it.

It was a month into my first year. Malcolm, a friend from my floor in residence, had an older brother named Chris, who lived with several guys off-campus. They invited Malcolm, my best friend Taz, and me to hotbox one weekend. I had only started smoking weed the month before; when I got high, the entire dorm floor came to my room to watch me laugh uncontrollably.

Chris had some cute roommates, and I wanted to impress them by handling my weed like a champ. We sat in their living room, talking about our first month at Western, as one of the guys crushed up the bud. I was feeling pretty calm about this— I could handle a joint. This would be easy.

But there was no rolling paper in sight. Another one of Chris's friends pulled out a big-ass glass bong from behind the sofa. He put it on his lap, scooped up the crushed weed, packed it into the bowl, then lit it up and took a hit.

I was mesmerized by the bubbling water and the thick white smoke trying to escape through the ice cubes in the stem. Everyone continued to chat as they took hits, and I participated in the conversation half-heartedly, trying to figure out how to get that thing up and running so I could avoid looking like an amateur.

Malcolm took his turn, then Taz. I watched her light the weed in the bowl. She leaned over, her long hair blocking my view, but a gurgling sound came from the bong. She pulled out the bowl and the smoke disappeared. She survived. But how the hell did she get her mouth over the opening?

As she exhaled, coughing and giggling, she passed it to me. It sat in my lap like a large rock. I looked down the stem—it was pretty big. Surely there was a trick to this. Only one way to find out.

I bowed my head towards the opening, then stretched my mouth as wide as I could to wrap it over the rim, wondering what kind of inhuman jaw structures they all had to be able to make it work.

"Lordamercy!" When I heard everyone start to scream and laugh, dropping to the ground one by one in fits of hysterics, I still didn't know that my mouth was supposed to go inside the stem, not around it. For the next three years, Chris and his room-mates called me Deepthroat Girl.

///

When it came to partying, I was a late bloomer. While the kids I went to Catholic high school with were getting trashed every weekend at house parties, I wandered the halls for the first year and a half, the lone Black emo kid. I wore black clothing, pink eyeshadow, and bows in my hair. I accessorized my school uniform with spiked rubber bracelets, and dyed my hair various shades of red. I carried around a photo album containing pictures of my favourite bands—Good Charlotte, My Chemical Romance, Fall Out Boy, AFI, From First to Last—that I'd printed out, wasting all the ink in my Lexmark.

By the end of Grade 10, I formed a group of equally outcasted girls: Shailene, a perpetually eye-rolling, indie biracial chick who couldn't escape the racist jokes of her new white boyfriend's friends; Arina, a badass transfer student, from an Armenian school, who had the latest Air Jordans; Jessa, a rich, progressive white girl with a bad attitude and a love of vampires and serial killers, and Tasmina—or Taz.

I met Taz in our second-semester science class. In the hallways, she smiled at me—reassurance that there were people who didn't think of me as a loner. At lunch, I'd see her leaning against the lockers with a group of science geeks, pretending to be interested in their at-home experiments, or sitting by herself and eating her home-cooked Indian meals. One of those days, I approached her.

"Isn't it the worst when you want to eat curry but it smells so strong?" I said.

"Yeah, I'm pretty tired of the white kids in the cafeteria complaining," she said with a weak smile.

"Wanna come eat lunch with us instead?" I asked her.

"I would love that."

We bonded over our brown families—both of us with overprotective mothers and lax father figures—and about how excited we were to get out of this teenage hellhole.

Together, the five of us hated everything about and everyone at high school: the hypocrisy of Catholicism, the gender roles that teenagers played into, the cafeteria politics, the school rules, the joke of a sex-ed curriculum, the shitty people. Adulthood was within reach; we just wanted to graduate and get out of there.

But we were also little feminists, unbeknownst to our own selves. Jessa and I found an escape in literature, and for our assignments we took up queer, feminist, and Black authors: Dionne Brand, Toni Morrison, Sapphire, Virginia Woolf, Jessica Valenti. We all refused to hold ourselves to men's standards, growing out our leg hair in defiance of the male teachers who stared at our legs as they scolded us for our short kilts. As the battle waged over kilt length, we hiked ours up higher.

We protested the patriarchy at all costs. We worked hard at the gym to get our bodies strong—a fuck-you to the boys who body-shamed muscular women. We bought lingerie to admire ourselves in, and gifted each other sexy underwear and pyjama sets for Christmas. We swore and smoked and burped out loud, and kissed each other in the back aisle of the movie theatre as our bags of beer stolen from home rested at our feet.

We were wholly unladylike and totally bored of our suburban teen existence. On weekends, I'd pick everyone up in my mom's '98 Honda Civic so we could go to the sex shop to buy condoms in case any of us ever lost our virginity. In the evenings after school we'd head to Jessa's house to watch *True Blood* reruns, nodding in agreement about the kind of relationship drama we wanted one day. When Obama was elected president, we skipped class and threw a dance party, jumping around in our bras and lace panties and swinging our kilts in the air. That a nation like America could elect someone who had spent their whole life on the outside felt reassuring to people like us—like we would one day find our place in the world too.

After graduation, we all went our separate ways, except for Taz and I, who together headed to Western. We wanted the keggers and wild house parties, dancing under strobe lights at all hours of the night, beer showers in lieu of champagne. I wanted partying to help me break out of my shy, painfully introverted shell, and so I immediately dove headfirst into any juvenile behaviour I could.

Residence was the perfect environment. Each weekend, there were parties on every floor. Fifteen or more people would cram into a tiny room to play beer pong, flip cup, or Centurion (a torturous game where you take a shot of beer every minute for a hundred minutes). Rooms were humid and sticky with body heat, as people danced and kissed and hugged and fell down while the vibration from loud music radiated through the furniture. Surfaces reeked of spilled vodka, rum, and coolers; spittle flew as drunk people slurred and shouted, pushed and shoved by others trying to get to the washroom to throw up. By 3 a.m., people were either passed out in bed or in the hall, or on the way to the campus hospital to get their stomach pumped. It was chaotic and messy, and to my surprise I fit right in, playing drinking games, perfecting my fist bumps and fist pumps (it was the era of *Jersey Shore*, yeah buddy!), dancing like a maniac in front of people I liked and trusted.

The lucky people who had a decent fake ID talked about the kinds of partying that took place outside of the university grounds. I couldn't find the ID of a Black girl anywhere in the vicinity, so I clung on to stories about epic parties from those who returned to tell the tale, waiting impatiently for my turn when I came back in the fall. Until then, most of what Taz and I knew about London was from reading "Outside the Bubble," a weekly flyer that people taped to bathroom stalls to let you know what was going on in the city.

We counted down the weeks until we moved out of residence for summer break, then the months until our nineteenth birthdays. When we returned in September, legal and ready to party at every bar in downtown London, we could only imagine what fun we'd get ourselves into.

///

I saw them the moment they entered the bar.

Three ghoulish figures, eyes glowing in the dark like nocturnal animals, floated towards us through the dense crowd of Halloween-goers. The hairs on my arm shot up. Every movement slowed and blurred, as if time and space had abandoned me. The bass from Ne-Yo and Pitbull's "Give Me Everything" vibrated through my body, but I couldn't hear the words.

I was at Jack's with Taz and Malcolm. We were finally in second year, and legal, and we wanted to spend our first adult Halloween at this charmingly dingy bar on Richmond Row that reeked of bleach and tequila. Dressed in expensive store-bought costumes, we threw back Jägerbombs from water-stained shot glasses.

But my excitement was short-lived, and my friends' was about to be too: as these bodies moved closer, eyes still on mine, I wondered how I could warn them about something I didn't quite understand myself.

The white people walked right up to Taz, Malcolm, and I, the only people of colour in Jack's. Three for three.

Dressed as cotton pickers, with overdrawn red lips, denim overalls, and straw hats with blond hair peeking out the sides, their faces were painted the most offensive coal black I've ever seen. A thin layer of unpainted white skin surrounded their inexpressive blue eyes.

Two guys and a girl stood before us in blackface, smiling smugly, mouths closed, not saying a word.

"What the hell is this?" My mouth had taken the lead before my mind was able to decide on the appropriate reaction, but they said nothing, only smiled.

Malcolm laughed so hard his drink spilled out of his mouth. "This is absurd," he said between gasps as he walked away.

Taz stifled her own laugh. But, I was growing angrier and more intimidated.

"Can't you talk? What the hell is your problem?" I yelled at the three people in front of me.

Still no answer. They continued to stare at me in silence, unblinking, leering. A bead of sweat trickled down my temple.

"You think this is funny? Say something!" My ears were ringing. Drunken bar patrons pushed past me and into the crowd. So many bodies around me—witnesses—yet no one stopped to help. All I could hear was my own voice screaming at these smiling white kids, with their black faces, to speak.

They looked back at me, composed, still smiling, daring me to lose my mind. I wanted the smug grins to dissolve off their faces, leaving behind remorseful tears. I wanted to give in to the humiliation and cry tears of my own. I wanted to join my friends and laugh until this no longer felt threatening, until this moment that should not still exist today was nothing but a distant, repressed memory.

I don't know how much time passed, but it felt like hours. Then, still smiling, they turned their black, painted faces and slowly disappeared into the crowd.

They moved on to their next victims, three South Asian people who had just arrived and were getting drinks at the bar. I made eye contact with the woman in that group, whose eyes, glassy with terror and pain, reflected my own. Then I looked away. I did not intervene; I couldn't. I turned my back and remained silent.

Something changed that night. My illusion of safety was shattered, and a feeling of deep discomfort made its permanent home inside me. It wasn't the first time I'd experienced racism since moving to London, but it was the first time it had been so malicious. What I didn't know was that it was only the beginning.

///

When I was seven, my mom dressed me up as a sexy French maid for Halloween. This sounds a whole lot worse than it actually was.

Fed on the sugary and fried treats of the '90s, I was big-boned and round all over, with cankles and paws for hands. If the Notorious B.I.G. and I had grown up together, I definitely would've been mistaken for him.

I was the first and only grandchild in twenty-two years. Everyone did their part to care for me. In the mornings, I woke up to my grandmother's cuddles and hugs, and a nicely packed lunch waiting to go. My mother dropped me off at school on her way to work. After my grandfather got home in the evenings, we'd lie on the couch watching TV as he cracked my knuckles—his way of showing affection. When he went to bed, my grandmother let me watch *Jerry Springer*.

I was spoiled; in my household, food was love, and my grandmother loved me dearly. On the weekends, I'd wake to the wafting smells of her cooking—nihari, ball curry, keema, potato balls—and murmurs of her gossiping on the phone with her sisters while sitting in her nightgown. Throughout the week, she indulged my every sugary, starchy desire—burgers, fries, McDonald's pizza, hot dogs, Kraft Dinner (wieners or it was trash), milkshakes, Dunkaroos, Lunchables, Teddy Grahams,

Mr. Noodles, Fruit Gushers, Nerds, Hubba Bubba, Bugles, Pillsbury Toaster Strudels—in large quantities, all day, every day. If I wasn't eating, I was overfeeding my Neopets and Tamagotchi to the point of food explosion.

By the time I was six years old, I was so large that we were shopping in the teen section to find clothes that fit me. And at my soccer finals, which I bombed by being both out of shape and having asthma, the cute teenage coach couldn't find a jersey that fit me. I held up the line as he, very nicely and with great discretion for a young man, found me something from the older girls' team. Our group photo tells the tale of a sad, Black girl in an adult-size, swamp green, cotton T-shirt, surrounded by all the cute little white girls in their beautiful, silky, emerald green jerseys.

What I really wanted as a seven-year-old was to be a mermaid for Halloween, but with my dreams of the sea crushed by a lack of size options, we scoured Party City at the last minute for something in the adult section that wasn't sold out. Hence: sexy French maid.

My mom thought it was quite fitting considering I went to a French Immersion school, and at this point, any humour was welcome. The costume came in a clear plastic pouch with a photo of a sexy, slim white woman taunting my too-young eyes with ideas of what women should look like. Inside the bag was a feather duster, a headpiece, an apron, and fishnet stockings, which we decided a second-grader could do without.

On Halloween, students gathered in the gym to show off their costumes by walking in a circle to the "Monster Mash" and "C'est l'Halloween" in the hopes of winning a prize. The teachers loved my punny costume, and I won first place. My reward was a bag of delicious treats and toys. I basked in glory as I walked back to my seat, but as I sat down, a bunch of my classmates jumped me, ripping my beautifully decorated bag wide open like hungry wildebeests, taking everything except for a small plastic pumpkin toy.

"You didn't deserve to win anyway, your costume wasn't that good," one of my snotty classmates said as he broke off a piece of my Kit Kat bar and chomped on it.

For the next decade, Halloween was tainted by this memory, and I spent my teens trying to find the perfect costume that would boost my confidence, wow my peers, and gain me entry into the world of cool-kid Halloween parties. I wanted the whole nine yards of sexy—latex, short skirts, high heels, too much makeup. I didn't want to be at a party with Regina George. I wanted to *be* Regina George.

I planned my costumes—a tight uniform of some kind; a sexy '80s housewife in leggings and a headband; a cute go-go dancer—but when it came time, I didn't have the confidence to pull them off. I just wasn't one of the hot girls.

But, during my first year at Western, I finally started to see myself differently. I followed eyes that scanned my body when I walked by, and my dormmates complimented the dresses I wore on the weekends. *You look soooo good. You look hot.* Here, I could be someone different. It didn't take looks to pull off a costume, it took confidence, and at a school infamous for partying, Halloween was the perfect opportunity to try again. In first year I was a hula girl, equipped with a grass skirt made of strands of green plastic, and a red tank top that I folded up to show my midriff. I felt so confident that, when second year started, Taz and I were both finally ready to conquer the "sexy" costumes.

In preparation for Halloween day, we hit the mall and found ourselves the sexiest costumes to blow our budget on. I bought a $75 Wonder Woman outfit and Taz chose Snow White (both unlicensed, because those are always more risqué).

When October 31st arrived, I stuffed my breasts into the tight cups of the red and gold corset and zipped up my red, shiny, six-inch-heeled, thigh-high boots. I put on my wristbands, attached my golden lasso, secured my cape, and slid my headband over my silky, straightened hair. I looked in the mirror; I had made it.

We both looked the part: me every inch a superhero, and Taz—with her perfectly heart-shaped face, rosy cheeks, and shiny, tousled jet-black hair—definitely a Disney princess. Now, as bomb-ass Wonder Woman and sexy Snow White, we felt confident and ready to present ourselves at the first of many epic Halloween parties. Broke from buying our expensive costumes, we walked to Jack's to meet Malcolm.

"Hey, Black Wonder Woman!" a white guy yelled from across the street. He was Woody from *Toy Story*.

"No, just Wonder Woman!" I yelled back, smiling through my teeth.

Taz thought it was hilarious. That was, until a green Power Ranger and his friends stopped us a block before the bar. The Power Ranger pointed at us. "Hey! Black Wonder Woman and Brown Snow White!"

"BITCH, IT'S JUST SNOW WHITE!" She was red in the face and wild-eyed in her poufy costume, ready to throw hands and start a princess-versus-superhero brawl.

The stunned Power Ranger was no match for the mother of dwarfs. He and his posse quickly moved along.

The taunts continued: *Black Wonder Woman? Look at Brown Snow White! Wrong colour, ladies.* I felt less like Regina George and more like a public spectacle. Taz and I eventually stopped responding, put our heads down, and walked as fast as we could.

People stood shoulder to shoulder at the bar, barely able to move. Plastic skeletons, cobwebs, and red string lights hung from the ceiling. On the dance floor, cute angels, sexy black cats, and a dozen other (white) Wonder Women danced with zombies, uniformed men, and Frankensteins. All around, white people were dressed in Indigenous-themed costumes, as Nicki Minaj (with a giant, fake ass included), and as Arab jihadists.

Behind the dance floor, Malcolm was waving with one hand and downing his Jägerbomb with the other. He was wearing a yellow onesie, abstract enough to have a stake in the festivities. We pushed through the sweaty bodies to get to him. He had already ordered us shots.

"Tonight is going to be epic," he said, clinking his glass with ours. I hoped to forget the walk over as we downed our shots, ready to finally experience the Halloween we had waited so patiently for. But as I set my glass down, I saw those three faces at the door—those glowing eyes already on me—moving past everyone and towards us, their target. There was nothing I could do.

///

In 2013, actress Julianne Hough wore blackface as part of her Halloween costume as Crazy Eyes from *Orange Is the New Black*. Actor Colton Haynes has dressed up in blackface on three different occasions. Comedians Sarah Silverman, Jimmy Fallon, and Jimmy Kimmel have all worn blackface on TV, and drag queens like Daytona Bitch and Charlie Hides have performed in blackface. Mindy Kaling's brother even wrote a book about it: he changed his appearance to look like a Black man in order to have a better shot at getting into medical school. Virginia governor Ralph Northam, Attorney General Mark Herring, and even Canadian Prime Minister Justin Trudeau have all been busted by yearbook or party photos showing them in blackface.

Blackface is also embedded in fashion. Magazines like

Vogue Netherlands, *Vogue Paris*, and *Numéro* have run photographs of white models painted in blackface. In the past two years, Prada had to pull a line of black monkey figurines with big, pronounced red lips that resembled the racist imagery of the Sambo stereotype, and Gucci removed a black turtleneck sweater from sale—it pulled up over the bottom of the face and featured an oversized red lip around the cut-out mouth.

Today's culture has evolved to include digital minstrel shows. Digital blackface—sharing a GIF or meme featuring a Black person (especially making exaggerated gestures or reactions) by someone who isn't Black, is a part of daily online and text communication. We've all seen non-Black people post side-eyeing Prince, eye-rolling Rihanna and James Harden, or an endless stream of Black reality stars, celebrities, and everyday Black people who end up as memes. Our expressions of emotion, too often perceived in real life as over-the-top and obnoxious, are reduced to looping videos as an emotional stand-in or for the comedic relief of others.

And that's what blackface is: the performance of Black stereotypes that reproduce negative portrayals of a marginalized group all for the sake of amusement. It doesn't have to be on a stage: modern-day minstrelsy includes non-Black people wearing urban wear and dreads, speaking in African American Vernacular English, appropriating clothing and hairstyles, and wearing foundation several shades darker or darkening skin tone on photos. (The Kardashian-Jenner clan is notorious for this, as well as appropriating Black women's hairstyles and ripping off ideas from Black designers for their own clothing lines).

While blackface has had a history in Canada since the mid-1800s, it has re-emerged on campuses in the last ten to fifteen years. Nearly every frosh week and Halloween, universities make national news when students throw parties involving cultural

23

appropriation and racist face-painting. In 2009, white students at the University of Toronto won a prize at a Halloween party for painting their faces brown and dressing up as the Jamaican bobsled team from *Cool Runnings*. In 2011, the Université de Montréal received backlash after people painted their faces in black paint during frosh week and dressed up as Jamaican sprinters, wearing the colours of the flag and speaking in mock Jamaican accents. In 2014, students at Brock University won $500 at a costume contest for also dressing up as the Jamaican bobsled team, black paint and all; and in November 2016, students at Queen's University held a racist costume party that encouraged students to dress up as foreign cultures. Students, mostly white, showed up as Rastafarians, Viet Cong guerillas, and Buddhist monks.

The motivating factor to dress in blackface can seem puzzling, but it's quite simple. For white people, blackface is a way to transform themselves temporarily, allowing them to indulge in and perform the Black mannerisms that they're itching to adopt—ones they try to get away with every day, like talking and walking "Black" or wearing cornrows.

For students, universities are spaces where young white people can act on both their greatest desires for Blackness and their most anti-Black fantasies. It's where performing stereotypes of Blackness becomes a social stepping stone—an easy way to break the ice, to make new friends, to win a prize, to get laid—at the expense of the targeted group. There is no concern for the impact on us, because we are seen as caricatures, bodies available to appropriate and mock. After the fact—if there's punishment at all—these acts are reduced to a debate over intent versus offence by school officials, or by the faux-intellectualizing of the right and others who don't see a problem. These excuses make room for white students to feel comfortable putting on black paint without consequences.

As an institution, university enables these behaviours by virtue of its mandate. The cushion between the real world and childhood, it serves as a place that encourages mistakes and risks—to dream big, to try and fail, to push the boundaries. And so it becomes a place to live out these desires and aggressions towards people of colour; to test the waters of white supremacy and the exploitation of free speech and expression—all without the same kinds of consequences that are experienced in the real world.

There's enough space to get away with these behaviours: these parties are often held off-campus, taking the responsibility off the schools. White students in particular just get a slap on the wrist—their behaviour is justified as youthful ignorance with a lack of malicious intent, in order to avoid risking their futures. Meanwhile, Black boys get suspended and expelled at disproportionate rates in elementary school and high school, meaning some of them don't even get the chance to go to university.

At the end of the night, those three students from Jack's went home, scrubbed the black paint off their faces, and went to bed. But who I am can never be washed away with soap.

///

That Halloween night at Jack's, Malcolm and Taz went to the dance floor, but I stayed by the bar, taking more shots to knock the bitter taste of old-school minstrel racism out of my mouth. "Great costume, girl," the man beside me said, a Chris Elliott lookalike in his forties dressed in the same Wonder Woman costume and Walmart boots. I laughed for the first time that night as he joked about his corset not fitting. Then he moved closer, his eyes shifting into a glassy, predatory gaze.

"You look really sexy in that costume," he said.

These were the words I had been waiting years to hear, but now I wished for nothing more than to be wearing a paper bag. His beer spilled all over my corset as he tried to kiss me. "Black Wonder Woman is the best!" he yelled from behind me as I left, wiping my face.

On the way back home from Jack's, Taz and I had no energy to respond to the comments about Black Wonder Woman and Brown Snow White. My costume might have won me a pass into the popular Halloween crowd, but fitting in was out of the question.

The reality that the city I had chosen for university was plagued by anti-Black racism would soon seep into every part of my academic and personal life. I would come to accept subtle and blatant racism as part of my existence. I would teach myself that survival meant looking over my shoulder when walking home at night, and maintaining my sanity often required drowning myself in alcohol and food. I would become both hardened and softened by racial hatred before I even knew how to love myself—before I even knew who I was. It wouldn't take long for me to realize that the best four years of my life would also be some of the worst, and that the fun, breezy university experience I had seen in movies featuring beautiful blond actors was not made for someone like me.

Though I was supposed to be a superhero that night, I didn't have the power to lift the weight of this new world that was crushing me.

That was the last year I went out for Halloween.

The Token in Class

WHAT TO EXPECT: You may experience the "classroom cooties"—an unexplainable, incurable phenomenon where the lecture hall could be completely full except for the seat beside you, and someone will *still* choose to sit on the stairs. Group projects will be your undoing: they heard Black students aren't high achievers, so they'll give you the easiest part of the project, like formatting the front page.

You may feel extremely uncomfortable with class conversations about racism or slavery. You may be asked, in front of everyone, if it's okay for the class to discuss these topics, as if you alone are responsible for the entire race of Black people. Students may not want to engage at all because they're scared that they'll hurt your feelings—or worse, that you'll call them a racist. They may say things like "Isn't talking about this divisive?" and "We're all human" and "I don't see colour." There will be one self-proclaimed "woke" white person who will try to bond with you by talking at length about all the ways Black people continue to be oppressed, when all you want to talk about are the ways you want Michael B. Jordan to oppress you.

HOW TO DEAL WITH IT: Acknowledge that, no matter how hard you scrub, you'll always have the token cooties in the classroom. So, kill them with your knowledge. Smile, but let that militant spirit twinkle in your eye. Trip them up by sitting in front of the class (they think you like the back row). Wear glasses; they won't expect that.

In group projects, there will come a time when your partners realize that you're a smart Black person and will start slacking. Throw them all under the bus by telling the prof about their unbecoming work ethic—the days of free labour are over. When the teacher singles you out and asks how we can all combat racism, tilt your head down and towards your left hand, point your index finger towards your temple, look her dead in her eye, and say, "By any means necessary."

token

Aside from Malcolm, I had only seen four Black people by the end of my first month at Western.

It was not a good start. I wanted to prove to everyone back home that the school I chose wasn't going to change me. They said I'd drown in a sea of white people, emerging an Oreo—a white girl in a Black girl's body—playing beer pong, wearing oversized sweaters and TNA leggings, and dancing like I had no rhythm. They hypothesized that I'd probably start listening to LMFAO (which I did) and join a sorority (which I did not).

I didn't want to prove people right, but it was starting to seem like I was becoming Black Becky. I had just about lost hope of finding people who looked like me when, on my way to class in November, I saw a Black girl on campus coming from the other side of the bridge I was about to cross. The bridge overlooks the Thames River, and she was headed south, away from campus and towards my residence, which meant she was probably a first-year too. But that was beside the point. She was here, and she was going to be my new best friend.

She was walking with her head up—good, the school hadn't broken her. Just a happy Black girl on her way back from class.

Our eyes met as we both stepped onto the bridge. She acknowledged me, so now I knew there was no way she could miss me. I slowed down.

We were mere footsteps away from each other now. In preparation, I raised my head a little higher and straightened my shoulders. I thought about all the things I would say to her. Maybe a smile or a hello, maybe take her aside and say, "Girl, I am *so* glad to see you," to which she'd reply, "Oh gosh, girl, me too. You have no idea," and we'd laugh and chat on the bridge about how the struggle is real and become lifelong friends. I imagined us sitting on the grass hill in front of the University College building in between classes, talking and laughing loudly on a shared blanket, ignoring all the scared and confused white people around us, just two Black girls in their Western bubble.

As we approached each other, our elbows nearly touching, I looked up, smiled right at her and waited for her eyes to meet mine.

Instead, she dropped her head and walked right past me, scurrying away, leaving me grinning into the ether like a psychopath.

I tried to piece the situation together in my head. She obviously saw me, but she'd also ignored me. As much as I wanted her to know I was here, in solidarity, I desperately needed some validation of my own that things would work out for us here.

A few weeks later, I saw another Black person on campus. I made eye contact and it happened again: eyes and head down, no acknowledgement. And then again. And again. It was as if they didn't want to be seen at all.

///

My choice to move hours away to go to Western was as shocking to my family as it was to me. I had no idea what university or college was even for, or why anyone would want to be in the school system longer than necessary. In Grade 11, when a provincial university representative came to our class to talk about our options for post-grad life, I shrunk into my seat as the kids around me conversed about majors and minors and campuses, things they knew about from their siblings or parents who had already gone.

No one close to me had braved the Canadian post-secondary system. My mother hated school and had gone into the work-force right after graduating. My father, a high school dropout, can barely read or write. My grandma was faced with the choices that many girls in Karachi at the time were given: support your family after grade school or get a degree. She chose to help her father. My grandfather got his degree at a college in Karachi and, though he would have liked to study more, he had to financially support his family, and then me.

"Have you given going to university some more thought?" he'd ask every time we went out to lunch.

"No, not really," I'd answer, and that was the truth. He wanted me to go so I could get a better job, but I couldn't think of any other perks. I planned to go into the workforce, like my mother. She didn't seem to mind it—after her shift, she came home, and had time to do whatever she wanted. But when my girlfriends started talking about the Ontario Universities' Fair, I decided to tag along.

At the Western table, a student rep from the Arts and Humanities department started explaining the program to me. I told her that I didn't want to go to university—I couldn't go through another several years being teased for sitting and studying alone. She looked at me like I was half stupid, half deserving of pity. "That only happens in high school," she said. "In university, it's cool to sit by yourself."

On the TTC ride back from the fair, I struggled to contain my huge smile. My two big plastic bags were ripped at the cor-ners, overstuffed with university viewbooks. My girlfriends sat in silence, more conflicted than ever about whether university was really for them. As for me, I was definitely going.

I wanted to be a writer, and the only English and writing programs that interested me were all the way at Western, in London, a city I hadn't even heard of until I read the brochure. To be practical, I opted to major in Social Work and to take a few English courses on the side, and I did more research into the school. Western was known for three things: quality education, school spirit, and partying. It was the place where keggers and raves happened, and all the other epic university fantasies that Canadian kids see in American movies about student life.

London was just far enough to get a fresh start, and I had the privilege of moving away for university. I worked on applying for scholarships to fund my residence and tuition fees, as well as my sales pitch to Taz: we both needed an adventure, and this was our chance.

Taz coming with me to Western almost didn't happen. Her mother, a strict, Catholic woman, didn't want her unmarried daughter to move away. She barely let Taz hang out with her friends, worried that they'd be a bad influence. But her mother's skepticism of the people around her daughter didn't extend to me. After school, she'd pick us both up and make me dinner, and later on, Taz and I would go upstairs to talk on MSN Messenger to boys from class we were crushing on. I was invited to every family event, and the kids called me "auntie." Taz and I had become like sisters, I had become part of their family. If her mom was going to let her go away with anyone, it would be me.

After endless fights and tears, and with one day left to accept the offer, Taz managed to convince her mother to let her go to Western. Her own pitch was that it had one of the best science programs in the country, and making her settle for anything less would hinder a successful career and marriage. Much to their annoyance, her parents couldn't disagree with that.

We were homesick our first few nights in Med-Syd, alternating between squealing over our new freedom and crying about how much we missed home. We immediately felt the isolation of our new environment: there were no other brown-skinned girls on our floor. By our fourth day, we hadn't made any friends yet; as we ate together in the cafeteria, questioning our decision to move two hours away from everything we knew, Malcolm approached us. Tall with a baby face, deep brown skin, small, deep-set eyes, and a buzz cut, he held his tray, also looking sad and pitiful.

"Can I sit with you guys?"

"Yes, of course," I said, moving my tray over.

Malcolm sat down and was quiet for a minute.

"So," he said, looking at Taz and me, then smiling. "It's just us." We laughed and laughed and laughed without saying a word, three brown bodies cackling in the near-white cafeteria like we were going mad.

Originally from Jamaica, Malcolm lived in a small, white town outside Toronto. As the only two Black people on our dorm floor, we bonded instantly. Along with Taz, we spent most of our days laughing obnoxiously at foolishness, hanging out in Malcolm's room listening to music, and sharing stories of the racism we'd experienced back home. Malcolm and I had both come to Western worrying about where we would fit in—if we would need to change to survive here. We already had, to an extent: we learned the lingo, like *biddy* (usually a white, hot girl) and *wheel* (to flirt). Malcolm anglicized his already-subtle Jamaican accent so he didn't have to deal with the terrible Caribbean impressions that people loved to do, and I found myself upping the vocal fry just to make myself relatable and unthreatening.

But in our rooms, we were unapologetically Black, playing hip-hop so loud that surfaces would vibrate, laughing obnoxiously, doing the Dougie and the Superman, and rapping to songs off Nicki Minaj's *Pink Friday* and Kanye West's *My Beautiful Dark Twisted Fantasy*. When we weren't screaming and hollering and being extra, we were sharing stories about our lives before we met each other. Most of our floor wanted to be part of the fun, joining us in our rooms to let loose or just to watch us enjoy ourselves. Others rolled their eyes. We annoyed them, we were *too much*. Some of the white girls stopped talking to us because our noise made them mad, totally oblivious to their own rowdy squealing on weekends. We didn't give a fuck what they thought, and instead we held on to being Black as tightly as we could.

/ / /

Kait spent her weekends out-drinking preppy kids who'd end up puking in house plants or passing out by the family pool. As her friends said, "There ain't no party like a Kait party."

She had lived in London her whole life. We met in our first-year Intro to Social Work class at King's University College, an affiliate school just a short walk from Western. She was a dark-haired pale-faced girl with wide brown eyes and a smile that took up her whole face—even if you were a stranger, she always looked happy to see you. We became friends by the second class, when our professor told us to pair up for an assignment, and all the King's students quickly rushed towards each other, leaving the two of us, both from Western, behind. Together, we studied at the library during weekdays and met up for coffee before class so I could hear her tales of the city. She was a party veteran thanks to her fake ID.

The week before second year began, I came back to London early. Kait already had a plan to get me white-girl wasted: Clarissa, her friend from high school, was having an end-of-summer party at her mom's house. Clarissa had been the hottest girl at their school—the epitome of white female beauty, a mix between Phoebe Tonkin and Megan Fox.

Our cab pulled up to a bungalow with a wood-panel exterior. Inside, above an old, floral cream couch, hung a taxidermied deer. The house was packed with people—all white, and mostly men. They slurred as they spoke, spilling beer on the carpet. I had never been to a house party before, though I had imagined it would look something like this.

These were local kids, and they definitely knew I wasn't from here. People stared as I walked through the crowd. In the kitchen, I stood beside Kait as she chatted with old friends. As I munched on chips, I caught a glimpse of a girl with long dark hair staring at me from the next room, her piercing blue eyes, rimmed with black eyeliner, were unblinking.

"Who's that?" I asked Kait. The girl was still watching me.

"Oh, that's Clarissa."

A tall, fit middle-aged woman with dyed blond hair in a tight dress approached us with a tray of Jello shots. "Oh, you're new! Are you a friend of my daughter?" She handed me a neon green shot.

"Actually, no, I'm just here with Kait," I said, thanking her.

"Well, you should really meet my daughter, she'll *love* you," she said, winking. Then she looked me up and down, took a shot, and continued her rounds.

As Kait and I made our way to the living room, I felt fingers brush softly through my hair. I turned around. Clarissa was peeking out from behind a wall, smiling at me. I caught up to Kait and followed her into the living room, which was full of guys in a colourful range of plaid shirts playing beer pong, yelling and cheering each other on. A few girls stood in the corner, watching their crushes, who were more focused on scoring a point than flirting with them.

"Hey everyone, this is Eternity," Kait said. A few people looked but said nothing, then went back to what they were doing.

I quietly went over to stand beside the pining girls, also pretending to watch. I was so uncomfortable. I could see how the token being here made other people feel awkward. I was *that* Black person who tagged along to one of their parties. They had to watch what they said, which songs they listened to. Even as the only person of colour, I knew how much space I took up just by being here.

Suddenly, one of the guys looked up at me. One by one, the rest of them fell silent as they also lifted up their heads. Self-consciously, I turned around, and Clarissa was right behind me again, her feline, electric blue eyes on mine, a smirk on her pink glossed lips.

"Hi, Clarissa," one of the guys said. She didn't answer—she didn't even look his way. She slowly lifted a hand up to caress my cheek, before putting it behind my neck. Her eyes didn't move.

"You are so beautiful," she whispered, pulling me into her, our lips gently colliding.

I don't know how much time passed, but it felt like minutes that Clarissa and I were kissing in the middle of the living room, surrounded by the guys who were in love with her and the women who loved them. When we finally pulled away from each other, the room was silent, and mouths were open. "We should hang out," she said, before turning around and slinking away.

I looked at Kait, hoping she wasn't regretting bringing me to this party. "That's my girl!" She high-fived me. "Now, let's get the hell out of here and go to The Barking Frog. These people are boring."

We had only been at the club for a few minutes when I spotted Sunil, the only other person of colour there that night. He looked at me, then walked towards us.

"Hey." Sunil smiled, his teeth glowing white in the darkness. "Wanna dance?"

We danced the rest of the night and exchanged phone numbers. Soon, we were spending our weeknights at bars with his friends, and our weekends listening to hip-hop. Originally from New Delhi, Sunil had come to London to pursue his dream of becoming a pilot. He was in his last year studying Aviation, and he had blown most of his OSAP loan for the year on partying. Though he was a few years older than me, Sunil expressed a kind of vulnerability that made him seem much younger—especially with his baby face and puffy cheeks, tall and lanky stature, and a pristine white grin that made his small, brown, almond eyes crinkle.

We shared our deepest secrets and trusted each other to keep them. Both having grown up in South Asian families, we had an unspoken cultural connection. We could snap at each other without the other taking it personally—the way I had seen my own cousins do to their spouses. We knew the same inside jokes about brown culture. He missed his mom back in New Delhi, so I tried my best to give him a taste of home. We'd make Indian food together—chana masala was our favourite. When he was feeling down, I'd surprise him with chai. In public, we made out just to scandalize the brown uncles and aunties who stared. He'd say words in Hindi and Urdu, thinking I wouldn't understand, then laugh in surprise when I'd respond in English.

But at night, in the middle of the dance floor, Sunil would pull his friends and me together in a huddle. "I never thought I'd be dating a Black girl!" he'd say, clinking his beer with everyone else's, like it was a cause for celebration. "It's true that once you go Black, you never go back. You should try it." Then he'd put his arm around me, pushing me forward. "Can you believe that she's Pakistani—and Black too?" When we got home, we'd fight about it. "It's a compliment. I don't know why you always get so mad," he'd say impatiently.

I thought only white folks could tokenize me. But Sunil and I were both South Asian. We were both from the same culture, and yet my brownness was negated by my Blackness. He was my reminder of my family back home; but to him, I was a story he could share with his friends about the Black girl he once dated. By early October, the phone calls fizzled out and we went our separate ways.

///

Megan was a little bitch. With her round, cherubic, freckled face, her Hunter boots and raspy voice, she was the epitome of a Western girl.

I was taking a second-year theory class with Professor Williams, one of the few Black professors I had during my years at Western. I could tell she was playing smart—you have to as a Black academic—leaving her pursed lips for when she thought the class wasn't watching. Sometimes, when I walked past her office in the department I heard her normally slow, deliberate speech quicken and a giggle emerge. I liked her, but she was especially curt with me. I understood, though: as the only Black person in her class, she wanted me to be her star student, to prove the others wrong, the way I'm sure she still had to with her peers. And yet she and her TA never cut me any slack. Unlike the rest of my courses, which I soared through with mid- to high 80s, I fumbled through Professor Williams's tough assignments without any of my usual academic finesse: I was getting low 60s in her class, the lowest marks of my second year. And even though it was my own fault, part me hoped she would help me out as the only Black girl in the class. But the message was clear: *I don't want you to fail, but I won't show you favouritism either.*

Megan sat two seats to my left and one row up. She was constantly talking to the girl beside her during the lectures, her annoying voice unable to successfully whisper. If she wasn't being disruptive, she was texting on her phone or smacking her gum.

For our last assignment, we had to get into groups. I looked around the room, and everyone had already settled into a team but me. "Eternity, why don't you join Megan's group?" Professor Williams said. Megan looked like I had taken a shit on her desk.

I wasn't happy about it either; still, I got up and joined the group, who fell silent and gave each other side-eye when I sat down. At our first meeting the next day, we sat in a circle, but they had all squeezed in until only my knee was included. I couldn't even get a word in as they talked about their ideas for which topic we should choose for the assignment and then delegated the work.

"Guys, I really need to get a good mark in this class," Megan whined. She looked at me. "Maybe you could do, like, the summary section. It should be easy."

"Sure, of course." I smiled and accepted my role as group dunce.

A few days before our Tuesday class, I caught a cold. I skipped, which Professor Williams had clearly warned us would drive down our grade, but I didn't want to go all the way to campus to get a doctor's note. That weekend, I gave in to Taz's pleas to go out on Saturday night. At the bar, I went to the bathroom to blow my nose, and as I was exiting, Megan walked in with her crew of girlfriends.

"Oh. My. God! Hey gurrrrl!" she squealed, her arms out-stretched as she hugged me. I reluctantly hugged her back, unsurprised by her intoxication-fuelled friendliness. "I didn't see you last class," she said, her eyes searching mine for some gossip.

"I wasn't feeling well," I responded. "I'm still sick, actually. I probably shouldn't be here."

As I spoke, I watched her lips curl into a grin. She put her hand on my shoulder. "Don't worry, I won't tell," she said, wink-ing. "Enjoy the rest of your night, gurrrrl. Have so. Much. Fun."

Next Tuesday, I was back in class working with my group, minus Megan. Professor Williams walked by my desk. "So glad to see you're feeling better and with us today, Ms. Martis," she said, trying to hold in her amusement. "I hope you had a great night at Jack's. Megan told me she saw you there."

Before I could answer, Professor Williams gave me a look I knew well: pursed lips, sassy eyes, a hand on her hip. I was mortified. Everything I needed to know was on her face: *You have to move better.*

I knew she was right. Black students have to work twice as hard in order to be seen as smart, and studious. Nearly half of U.S. undergraduates today are students of colour, but Black students are still lagging behind, especially at elite schools. (Canada doesn't collect race-based data, so we don't have these numbers.) They also have a higher dropout rate, which research has attributed to feeling there's an implicit bias by faculty and the school towards white students, not seeing peers who look like them, being unable to find community, financial issues, and experiencing discrimination and racism at school or by faculty and students.

In another class, with another professor, Megan's little tat-tle could have affected my academic performance. She had gone out of her way to make sure she ratted on me. But I wasn't surprised. I knew how white girls operated: smiling in the faces of women of colour, acting like our friends and allies, calling us "queen" and "girl" and snapping their fingers; then turning on us for personal gain—using tears, or carefully chosen words disguised as false innocence or concern, to plant seeds that they can reap for their own benefit.

When Megan missed class or texted or had conversations about her weekend instead of listening to the lecture she paid for, that was not my business, nor my money. When her friends skipped class, she took notes for them. When I skipped class, she took notes for our professor. She was policing me, and she used it as her one-up, as if it were her job to report and weed out the bad, lazy students who were not devoted, who didn't belong.

If Megan felt bad, she didn't show it. Instead, she was friendlier than before—stopping by my desk at breaks to make one-sided small talk, asking if I wouldn't mind sharing my notes with her for the class she had skipped once again. All the while, I worked on putting together the best damn summary a dunce could. And when Megan stopped showing up to class and our group meetings altogether but was posting plenty of Facebook selfies in her party outfits, the irony was not lost on me—or Professor Williams when I went to her office hours to speak to her about it. "Oh, I'm very aware, Ms. Martis," she said, raising an eyebrow. "I'll give each group member an individual grade instead."

During the last class of the semester, Megan showed up to submit her assignment. As Professor Williams gave her final remarks, Megan looked up from her phone and raised her hand. Everyone turned to her.

"Sorry to interrupt, but I just wanted to thank you all for teaching me so much this year," she said, squeezing a tear out of her eye. "I'm from a small town just outside of London, and Western has really opened my eyes to all different kinds of people. I had never seen people who weren't white—well, except for a few Asians in my town. Until this class, I thought that Natives ran naked in the bushes."

Professor Williams and I made brief eye contact, and the corners of our mouths twitched. "Thank you for sharing that, Megan," she said slowly. Satisfied with herself, Megan went back to her phone.

At the end of class, the professor handed out the graded rubrics, each of us getting our own mark. Megan stormed out, and I could hear her whining, raspy voice on the verge of tears in the hall, complaining about her unexpected, unfair, low 60. I looked down at my own rubric. I'd gotten a 75.

///

The inside of a London Transit bus is very blue. It has bright yellow poles, too, so it feels as if you're riding around in a giant submarine. London buses are also crowded with strollers, walkers, and students' backpacks. It's rare that a seat is left vacant.

On my way downtown during rush hour, I took a seat in the middle of the bus.

I looked around: all the other seats were taken, except for the one beside me. More people piled on at the next stop. They looked at the empty seat, then remained standing. Across from me, two men alternated between looking at each other, then at me, smirking. I averted my eyes, focusing on the yellow poles.

At the next stop, several more people got on as everyone shifted uncomfortably, trying to make room. The seat beside me was still vacant. Was my winter jacket spilling onto it? But across the aisle, people were jammed into the four seats, seemingly unbothered by the tight squeeze and puffy coats.

On the PA, the driver irritably asked people to move right to the back of the bus. As people slowly shifted towards the tail end, a Black girl approached the seat beside me. She looked around for another, then back at it—all without looking my way—before reluctantly sitting down.

I was in third year by then, and at this point I knew better than to turn to her and crack a smile, so we both looked forward, reading the bus advertisements. Why hadn't I ever noticed the poles were caution-tape yellow? I looked at the two men across from us again. They were whispering now as they leered.

I knew she felt the humiliation. The only two Black people on this bus were sitting beside each other, and we would've done anything to avoid this, to not become the centre of attention for something that would have been normal back home.

A white woman in her early fifties with a dark-brown pixie cut was holding the pole in front of us. She looked down at us, smiling.

"Are you two related?"

I felt the girl beside me stiffen. I paused, wondering if she would respond. She tilted her head slightly towards me, like she wanted me to speak for both of us.

"No," I said assertively.

"Oh," the woman stuttered, slightly embarrassed. She turned her body to face the back of the bus. I turned my head towards the girl beside me. She still wouldn't look at me, but there was now a faint smile on her face.

The longer I lived in London, the more I came to understand why that girl on the bridge and that girl on the bus didn't want to make eye contact. Most public space is white space. Parks, museums, schools, neighbourhoods, restaurants—places with middle-class values—are still predominantly accessed by white people. Non-white bodies are hypervisible and heavily surveilled in these spaces. If we want to pass through without trouble, we have to appear non-threatening. We have to dress, speak, and act in ways that are compatible with the other people in these spaces.

University is one of these white, middle-class spaces, and Black students have been policed and singled out as being "out of place" on campuses across North America. In May 2018, a white student called the police on a Black Yale student who was taking a nap in her own dorm's common room. In August, a Smith College employee called the police on a Black student who was eating lunch in the common room. In October, a Black student at the Catholic University of America was approached by police officers after a white campus librarian called 911. She claimed he was argumentative, though she wouldn't tell officers why she denied him entry into the library in the first place. In November, a white professor at the University of Texas San Antonio called the police on a Black student for doing what all students in hours-long classes do: putting her feet up on a chair. In April 2019, a Black Columbia University senior was pinned down by security officials near the Barnard campus library. Students are supposed to show ID after 11 p.m., but students say this isn't usually heavily enforced.

A gathering of Black bodies makes us even more visible, more susceptible to being targeted. When groups of Black students hung out together on campus, we were stared at with fear and loathing. Black laughter—Black *joy*—put people on edge.

Alone, we stood out on and off campus, but a group of us was asking for trouble. Acknowledging other Black people— being seen with them—validated our tokenness, and raised suspicion. We all contributed to making each other feel even more invisible by ignoring a friendly smile, but the alternative was worse: to make eye contact with one another was to alert the whole campus or public space that there were two Black people in the same spot. And they were all watching, waiting for us to acknowledge each other. It was direct proof that we were out of place, and a dilemma that had no solution: when you are so desperate for connection with people who understand your struggle, how do you reach out when the act of connecting in public puts you both at risk?

When groups of white girls laugh or hang out in a public space, nobody feels threatened. Nobody thinks to call security or the police. Same with white men—in fact, rowdiness and taking up space is expected. Frat and sorority parties are obnoxious and loud, but that is mitigated by small fines for noise or by moving these groups into neighbourhoods where they can continue to make noise. But the noise and space Black people take up in public comes with greater consequences.

In 2014, Michael Dunn was sentenced to life in prison with no chance of parole for shooting and killing Jordan Davis, a seventeen-year-old Florida high school student who wouldn't turn down the Lil Reese song playing in his friend's SUV. In August 2015, a book club of predominantly Black women was kicked off a Napa Valley Wine Train tour after they were deemed to be laughing too loud. They've since settled an $11 million racial discrimination case against the complainant.

Events that Black folks attend have had their licences revoked or cancelled because of noise complaints from citizens and city councillors. In 2015, the City of Toronto tried to limit Afrofest's two-day permit to one day because of noise complaints, then took it back after social media criticism—and admitting they only received eight. In 2018, Carnival Kingdom's soca party in Vaughan, Ontario, one of the biggest music events during Carnival weekend, was cancelled with less than two hours' notice because of complaints made before it even began. In England, residents living near the Notting Hill Carnival in London have complained about it being too loud and rowdy, which has led to the use of decibel readers by city officials to police volume levels.

It wasn't long before I started doing the same thing as that girl on the bridge. I would spot another Black person from afar, eager for acknowledgement, then instinctively turn away. In my last two years, after meeting more Black students, I learned that they were also guilty of ignoring each other. We were all scared and exhausted; being a token had reduced us to nothing more than bodies to police. It wasn't about hiding—we were the most visible people around—it was about survival. About doing no more than simply passing through as quickly as possible.

We all could have broken the unspoken code of silence—the climate of fear that kept the vulnerable isolated from one another, away from the chance of connection and friendship. Perhaps it was solidarity enough that we were at this school, in this chaos, together. Maybe that was all we could give each other at the time. Because that's how people work under systems of oppression: the best way we can.

The Token Gym Rat

WHAT TO EXPECT: People will want to see if you work out differently. They will examine you for superhuman strength to see if you're fast like your native countryman, Usain Bolt. In the change room, women will try to catch a glimpse of your breasts or vagina to see if it differs from theirs.

Men will look at your junk to see if you live up to the hype.

HOW TO DEAL WITH IT: Be sympathetic towards your change room chums! Some of them have never seen token parts in their lives. But that doesn't mean you can't toy with them. Pretend to lower your towel repeatedly and watch their heads twist until they have whiplash. When you get out of the shower and they're anticipating full naked glory under your towel, drop it dramatically only to reveal your undergarments. Tell them you know Usain personally and that you were part of the Jamaican bobsled team a few years back. Don't be surprised if someone asks for your autograph.

go
back
to
your
country

"Eternity," my mother's friend Angela said sternly, taking a sip of the Tim Hortons coffee she held in one hand as she pointed at me with the other. My mom and I were sitting on milk crates in her garage, as we did most nights—the two of them with their caffeine and cigarettes, and me with my chocolate milk. "If anyone calls you a nigger, you break their fucking nose." She then proceeded to take my hand and show me the exact force I would need to accomplish this assault.

I wasn't yet eleven.

Angela made me practise over and over, readjusting my flexed wrist, reminding me what part of the nose would need to come in contact with the heel of my palm for maximum damage.

If anyone was going to teach me how to do a palm strike, it was Angela. She was a butch lesbian, and not out to her Catholic mother, who was still trying to find a good boy for her thirty-something-year-old daughter. I didn't know what the word nigger meant or why I would need to hurt someone who said it. I looked to my mother for clarity, but she remained silent. Angela sensed my confusion. "Nigger is said by people who hate other people because of the colour of their skin," she explained.

My mother's silence was indicative of the rest of my family's position when it came to talking about my multiracial heritage. They had never called me mixed or Black—or anything. When my mother spoke to people about my background, she never said *I* was Jamaican, but that my father was.

I arrived at the intersection of two brown families from different castes and ethnicities. My maternal grandfather is the son of Mangalorean parents but was born and raised in Karachi, Pakistan. He and his five siblings grew up without money; their father—my great-grandfather—was a cook for a well-off family that paid him ten cents a day. They didn't have necessities like food or shoes, nor luxuries like a camera to capture memories. As a child, my grandpa loved reading the news but couldn't afford a newspaper, so he'd take the neighbours' off the porch in the morning then return it before they woke up. To this day, he still wakes up at 5:30 a.m. to read the newspaper. My great-aunts and great-uncles were put into arranged marriages, but my grandfather fell in love with my grandmother, an Anglo-Indian woman who was a fellow member of a youth leadership group in Karachi. And, against his parents' wishes, he married her.

Anglo-Indians in Pakistan were people of both Indian and British parentage (also known as Eurasians), as well as Brits living in India. My grandma's mother was Pakistani and her daddy was an Irishman who was left in Karachi by his father after World War Two. Anglo-Indians had a bad rap in Pakistan. At the time of independence, there were about 500,000; many gained the distrust of Indian nationalists over their decision to identify with British rule. They also had a reputation of being partygoers and drinkers, always entertaining and living lavishly.

When my grandparents got married, they merged two families that had no business being together. Years later, much of our family on both sides made Canada their new home. At the parties that my grandmother hosted every Sunday, my grandfather's family would sit on one side of the house, looking on quietly at my grandmother's gregarious relatives.

There was whiteness in the family, but no one was prepared for a Black child—I had shaken up the family dynamic in a new way. At home with my family, I would sing along to songs from my favourite Bollywood film—*Kuch Kuch Hota Hai*, starring the dreamy, never-aging Shah Rukh Khan. I wore langas to weddings. My grandmother's cooking, a reminder of Karachi, brought our displaced and homesick family together on Sunday afternoons, when my uncles and aunts addressed me by Urdu or Konkani terms of endearment as they pinched my cheeks. When my grandmother took me to her favourite Indian grocery store, the owner never looked at me any differently. At family parties or community events, I never felt out of place. Even at our favourite South Asian restaurants, they greeted me like an Indian child: *How are you, beta?*

But I was the odd one out—a brown-skinned girl with big curly hair. Even as different ethnic groups poured into the city, my family had their work cut out for them with a half-Black kid, and my father wasn't around to help us understand my Jamaican heritage. While the '90s saw the emergence of the mixed-race movement, biracial people were hard to come by. My tan-skinned, straight-haired mom and grandmother would drive to Buffalo, New York, just to find books with characters I could look up to, and dolls that looked like me.

///

Even in her late twenties, my mother didn't have a wrinkle or fine line in sight—she could easily have passed for a teenager. By then, she was rocking tattoos along her arms and chest and piercings on her face, accompanied by bleached blond hair and pink lipstick—Snob by Mac was her favourite. She wore fitted Tommy Hilfiger ensembles and bandanas, and she was always yelling over the phone at some man who was five minutes late for their date, then counting down the time until he came back grovelling. I adored her beauty, brawn, and badassery. I was so happy to be hers. When we were together, I would wonder if I made her feel uncool.

When Amazing Amy came out in Canada, my mother couldn't stop talking about how they had a Black doll. She stood in line to get me one, in its massive green box. Amazing Amy was all the rage; she came with different kinds of food that you could feed her, and different outfits. Black Amy was so pretty: cute little burgundy lips, deep brown skin, and curly black hair like mine. She was annoying with her constant whiny demands, though, so I fed her liver, which she hated, as payback.

I understood that Black Amy and I had the same skin colour and the same curly hair, and I knew that I looked different than my grandmother and mother. But I didn't see that difference as division yet—we were just different shades. During arts and crafts time in kindergarten, I drew myself and my grandfather in brown crayon, and the rest of my family in peach. We were still a family, but in an assortment of body sizes and colours.

By Grade 2, I began to realize there *was* a difference associated with our skin colours. In my grandmother's soaps, all the airtime went to the white (or, as I called them, peach) people, like Sharon Newman, the beautiful heroine on *The Young and the Restless*, who was blue-eyed with straight blond hair. In the tabloid magazines we kept in the house, peach people graced the covers. At school, I noticed the way teachers doted on the cute little peach girls but not me; and how their cheeks turned a magical shade of pink in the winter, the way my grandmother's did, but mine couldn't, no matter how long I stood in the blistering cold. I watched the way my mother's hair, silky and dyed blond, flattened like spun gold as she ran the straightening iron through it in preparation for a night out. I was mesmerized as she applied makeup to her flawless face; when she left for the night, I'd press my finger in her Mac Studio Fix powder and run it across my hand—an astounding contrast, like chalk on a blackboard.

My mother and grandmother were both closer to peach. But I was closer to darkness, and darkness was danger. Darkness was when I ran back into the house, smelling like the outdoors after playing with the kids on the block all day. It was when bad men drove around to lure little children into their cars when asking for directions. It was when the Boogeyman under the bed made his move. Without realizing it, I had internalized a dislike of myself that I couldn't articulate.

/ / /

The first time my family had to address my Blackness was at my cousin's house when I was nine. It was a party, and a young boy, distantly related to my cousin, came downstairs to the basement to play video games with the rest of us. He backed out of the room the moment he saw me. "She's Black! I don't want to play with Black people," he yelled as he pointed at me. I told my grandfather what he said, and my grandpa confronted the boy's parents. We never spoke about it again.

Later that year, I became best friends with two Lebanese girls who lived down the street. They called me Black all the time; I didn't know why that mattered, but I knew I felt uncomfortable. I felt the reluctance of their father, too, when I came over for dinner. He could barely look me in the eye. When they invited me over during their family parties, the adults walked past me like I didn't exist. One day, their baby cousin was over, staring at me, thumb in mouth as I waved. "She's scared of Black people," her sister said. My mom gave their parents a proper schooling, and that was the end of the conversation.

My mom and I never discussed our contrasting features, even when I became a teen and servers started asking us if we wanted separate bills. Not even when she talked to strangers about her daughter and they asked "where is she?" as I her look-alike stood right there. And she didn't feel the way I did when it came to my appearance. Boys didn't turn her away because she was too dark. She wasn't followed around department stores by old white ladies. She didn't have to feel uncomfortable or nervous in the spaces white people inhabited. The small fraction of whiteness I inherited was nowhere near enough to pass like her.

My father's name was rarely mentioned in our house, unless I asked. And even then, my mom gave me one-sentence answers. But I wanted to know what his identity contributed to my own. What did it mean to have a Black father? How could I bridge these two identities harmoniously? If he was out of the picture, did I have a right to call myself Jamaican? Could I be both— Black but still brown, brown but also Black?

To the mothers of my Black girlfriends, I *was* Black, and the percentage didn't matter. When we turned thirteen and started going to the mall on our own for the first time, it was their families who taught me about my rights in case the police stopped me, about what stores sent security guards after Black kids, and what to say if I was falsely accused of shoplifting. Women like Angela, like these mothers, were the ones who first taught me how to navigate the world as a Black person, before I even knew what that would mean.

/ / /

On my first day of high school, I took a seat beside another Black girl and got out my notebook. She stared at me intensely. I looked back at her, feeling insecure, but she didn't break eye contact.

"What's your background?" she asked.

I repeated what my mother always told people. "My mother is Pakistani and Irish and my dad is Jamaican." The girl stared at me for a few seconds longer, nodded, turned back around.

This question became the main interaction I had with the other Black girls in high school, and each time it was just as uncomfortable. I dreaded the pressure to describe myself in a few words, to decide what to include or exclude, of not feeling confident in my incomplete answer.

But in a school full of teens who were also thinking about the nuances of their identities, I could start to think about my own. "Light skin" and "dark skin" teams were emerging, and kids put an *ls* or *ds* beside their Facebook names. People wore their ethnicities with pride through their clothing, or expressed their multiracial identities in the bios of their Facebook pages, calling themselves *mixed*. The lighter you were, the more attractive; the less conventional your mix, the more desirable. *Mixed* wasn't a word I liked; and anyway, it was usually reserved for white-Black or white-Asian biracial people. But it was what the Black kids called me. Everyone else referred to me as Black; the brown kids, though accepting of our shared ethnicity, couldn't get past my appearance.

I felt the pressure to identify a certain way to the brown and Black kids, desperate to be accepted by at least one side. I felt like a fraud during cultural food week when my mom brought me sweet jalebis to sell at the Pakistani table. I was too embarrassed to be asked why a Black girl was selling Indian sweets and not Caribbean food, so I ate them all by the end of second period and then bought some pierogis from the Polish kids.

How could I feel closer to being Black when I knew nothing about my own father? Was including my mother's whiteness in my own identity necessary or excessive? Would I be accused of trying to distance myself from my Black side simply because I mentioned I was also brown? Was it a betrayal to my family to feel closer to being Black than Pakistani? How could I only call myself Pakistani but not consider how being Jamaican was the reason for my appearance, my dilemma of fitting in, that self-defence lesson from Angela?

In Grade 11 chemistry lab, one of the popular Black girls walked over to my station. "Where are you from?" Her question caught me off guard; by now, most people already knew. I paused for a few minutes, wanting to say I was Black. I thought about leaving it at "mixed."

I used my default answer, hoping it would be sufficient: "My mother is Pakistani and Irish and my dad is Jamaican."

She laughed. She laughed and laughed and pointed at me, gasping for air as I waited to see what was so funny. Finally, she caught her breath. "You're a terrorist," she said, before erupting in another fit of laughter. She pointed at me again. "Terrorist! Terrorist! Terrorist!"

///

Shut the fuck up, nigger.

It was my third year at Western, and my then-boyfriend, Amir and I were walking back to his car after a late-night study session at the University Student Centre. It was a frigid fall night and the campus was empty, except for two young white guys who were walking up the hill towards us. They must have been first-years: very drunk, wearing dress shirts and no jackets, and coming from the direction of a residence.

The blond one, flushed with intoxication, asked if there was anywhere at this hour to get food.

"The Student Centre is still open," Amir said.

"Shut the fuck up, nigger," the blond hissed at him.

"Excuse me?" I searched his expression to make sure this wasn't a joke. My right hand started shaking. *Flat palm. Maximum damage.* Rage blinded me and darkness framed my vision. My heart was beating hard against the wall of my chest, my ears were ringing. I could barely hear Amir telling me to ignore this boy with his neatly coiffed hair.

"I said, shut the fuck up," the guy repeated, then turned to me. "And you, go back to your country, you bitch."

His friend held him back as he stalked closer, his arms flailing and feet stumbling over each other.

"Yo man, what's wrong with you?" his friend whispered to him, his own eyes widened in fear.

"I was born here," I said as I kept walking. I laughed—it seemed like the appropriate response to calm the fight-or-flight instinct that was threatening to take over my body.

"Fuck off, you Black bitch," he slurred. "Your boyfriend is a nigger, and I'm going to beat the shit out of you."

He charged at me as he continued his threats, his friend desperately clinging to the fabric of his shirt. From Amir's protective grasp, I yelled back at the blond that he was ignorant.

The boy's yells turned to screams so piercing he was losing his voice. *Go back to your country, bitch. Nigger, bitch, third-world, kill you* . . . Finally, his friend, apologizing profusely, was able to pull him towards the Student Centre.

Silence returned, but I could hear my heart beating in my ears. I looked at Amir.

"Aren't you angry?" I was exasperated.

Amir shrugged. "I'm used to it."

Amir didn't flinch at being called a nigger. Each time he walked up the stairs to my off-campus apartment, white women looked on, terrified, watching him until he was out of sight. Clicks of locking car doors followed him when he walked down the street. Arabs, who didn't realize they shared a language, would make racist comments.

Driving a cab in London night and day, he experienced some of the worst verbal abuse I'd ever heard. People refused to get into the car because they didn't want to be driven around by an immigrant. An older woman once hit him with her purse because he wasn't a white driver. At night, most of his customers were students. White girls asked if the stereotypes about Black men were true. Sometimes they mocked his English. Men started fights about paying the fare, threatening to beat Amir up when he refused to answer their ignorant questions. The police were always getting called to defuse situations.

Sometimes, he kept me on speakerphone to listen to the conversations that took place in his cab. One night, I heard a drunk couple get into the backseat.

"Your accent is so exotic," the guy slurred. "Where are you from?"

"I'm from Bombaclat," Amir told them dryly.

"Bombaclat," they both repeated pensively. "Is that near Kingston?"

The day after the incident with the two white guys near the Student Centre, I went to campus police to file a report, empowered by the school's zero-tolerance policy for discrimination—something that had stuck with me from the open-house tour years back. Days later, an officer brought me in for an update. I sat in a small dim room with a bright light in between us, like I was being interrogated.

"We've looked into this and I wish there was more we could do, but there are no cameras around that area, so it's impossible to identify these two boys." He looked sympathetic.

"So what happens if that guy does this again?" I asked.

"Well, hopefully someone will report it and we'll be able to get him then." I thought about all the surveillance around the campus. How could there be no cameras in one of the busiest areas? Worse, how could an incident of this magnitude be dropped just like that, only to let it happen to another person? By then I had experienced a host of issues in the city and on campus that I'd handled myself, even when the weight of carrying it alone felt enormous. The one time I had asked for help, nothing could be done.

/ / /

Western is known for its welcoming and lively campus, full of activities and school spirit, but like other schools around Canada, it has its share of hate incidents and crimes that go largely unmediated by officials. After all, Western is the school that employed the late psychology professor Philippe Rushton, a man who was part of the legacy of scientific racism and research into race-based intelligence. Under the security of tenure, Rushton carried out studies that used brain and genital size to claim that Black people were the most unintelligent and hypersexual of all races. He was employed at the university from 1977 until his death in 2012.

While I was a student, friends shared their stories about the word "nigger" scribbled in trees, on walls in residences, and on campus property. About being mocked, both on campus and off, for the way they spoke. About the microaggressions they faced from strangers and peers. They recalled white students having "discussions" on whether racism was still real, and professors asking them specifically if the class could talk about it. In my last year, a young Black girl was allegedly mocked for the way she spoke and kicked off a bus by a driver who said her presence was "threatening," yet no witness could confirm his statement. People who knew her described her as a gentle soul.

In classrooms, white students took up time to share their thought process on racism out loud and then thanked us for giving them the space to learn about other cultures for the first time. When a course had a module on race, seats were noticeably empty that week. The following class, students gave *me* their excuses for why they skipped, then asked to borrow my notes. During a discussion on race in my third-year Literary Criticism course, a white girl who was always on her phone and talking loudly in class punched her hand into the air. "Like, I don't get why we're still talking about slavery," she said with annoyance. "Like, it's done. Get over it." Thankfully, no one agreed with her.

But she wasn't alone in feeling attacked by conversations about race. A year after I graduated, the *Gazette*, Western's student newspaper, published its first Black History Month issue. To show the amount of hate that students sent in because of the issue, the editor at the time, a woman of colour, published one of the letters the paper had received: "Why does it seem that the point of Black History Month has changed from celebrating Black culture to making white people feel bad for being white?" In February 2015, a student hacked the Recreation Centre's Twitter account and posted a tweet that said, "Fuck all niggers." It was taken down and the university apologized. The following year, white students made national headlines when they posed in front of a "Western Lives Matter" banner. (While the school initially condemned this, it ultimately decided that it didn't violate Western's code of conduct.)

Many schools do condemn racist and discriminatory actions of students, but punishment is enforced to varying degrees, from expulsion, suspension, or a warning. Often, it's chalked up to a "learning opportunity," while those targeted don't even get a quarter of the support and resources that perpetrators do in order to move forward from the incident.

Canadian students aren't filing racial discrimination complaints, because they fear they won't be believed, or because they ended up resolving the issue on their own outside of a formal complaint. Other times, it's because they don't know where to go on campus for help. The root issue is the same: students do not trust that their school will do anything to help them.

Many post-secondary schools across the country report hate incidents on campus in the single digits, if they keep track at all. And there are so many hate incidents that police can't follow through on, like with my own complaint, so these don't get included in the data. Other reports may not even be considered a hate incident or crime by police. This means we don't have an accurate account of just how prevalent this is on university grounds.

The police couldn't help me, and there were no human rights complaints that I could have filed, no charges to press when someone spewed the kind of hate that made me afraid, because there are no criminal laws against these increasingly common incidents. And things have not gotten better since I graduated. The past few years have seen an alarming rise in white nationalism on Canadian campuses.

The alt-right, or alternative right, is a poorly defined group comprising white nationalists, white supremacists, nativists, populists, anti-Semites, Holocaust-deniers, incels, neo-Nazis, neo-fascists, and others. It's popular with young men, and supporters are often found in the dark corners of the internet and online forums, including 4chan and 8chan. Some of its signature tactics are memes and cyber harassment. It also has more women at the helm, even though it's just as misogynistic and anti-feminist as other far-right movements. Its members are often young, educated, and articulate, making it ideal on university campuses, hotspots of critical thinking and freedom of expression, and for students looking to express thoughts that would otherwise be deemed politically incorrect or racist.

Students in Toronto organized a "U of T Rally for Free Speech" event in October 2016 with Jordan Peterson, a psychology professor who was the subject of protests over his refusal to use a student's gender-neutral pronouns, and former right-wing Rebel Media employee Lauren Southern. In March 2018, Wilfrid Laurier University allowed white nationalist and soon-to-be failed Toronto mayoral candidate Faith Goldy to give a talk entitled "Ethnocide: Multiculturalism and European Canadian Identity," but it was cancelled when a student pulled the fire alarm. Free speech groups have also formed at several universities, including York, the University of British Columbia, and Concordia.

As each year goes by, alt-right incidents across Canadian campuses gain more visibility. In 2015, a number of white pride flyers promoting a white student union called the Students for

Western Civilisation were put up across Toronto universities. In September 2016, on the University of Alberta campus, Sikh students were targeted with posters that said "Fuck Your Turban" and "If you're so obsessed with your third-world culture, go the fuck back to where you came from." Two months later, flyers posted on McMaster's campus and in downtown Hamilton read "Tired of Anti White propaganda? You are not alone." Two weeks after that, posters with anti-gay, anti-Muslim images and the phrase "Make Canada Great Again" were found on McGill's campus.

In February 2017, posters denying the Holocaust were found at the University of Calgary campus. In September, recruitment flyers for alt-right group Generation Identity, which has a large presence in Europe, showed up on several Canadian campuses. That same month, two campuses in Fredericton were targeted with alt-right posters, including three on a Maliseet welcome sign at St. Thomas University that read "Critical thought is a crime," "Equality is a false god," and "We have a right to exist" alongside an image of two white people and a link to an alt-right website.

In November 2017, the University of Victoria was postered with alt-right flyers encouraging people to "Defend Canadian heritage" and "Fight back against anti-white hatred." Alongside links to alt-right websites, the poster also read "((((Those))) who hate us will not replace us" (triple parentheses are commonly used by neo-Nazis to identify Jewish people). Later that month, the University of Regina and U of T were postered with flyers that read "It's okay to be white." Weeks later, stickers and posters promoting white supremacy sprung up around Brandon University's campus. In November 2018, posters that also said "It's okay to be white" were posted on the Fort Garry campus at the University of Manitoba and faxed to the Women's and Gender Studies department. In October 2019, a racist and homophobic note was posted inside a dorm at Queen's University, threatening to "scalp you all" and "make you bleed." The list goes on and on.

How can the imaginary, perceived threat to whiteness—the fear of losing the privileges and comforts associated with being white—be ripped away simply because of "diversity," when every system has defended and upheld whiteness ferociously for centuries? And yet those who fear that whiteness is under attack then attack people of colour in the form of threats, violence, and harassment. Those who defend their right to freedom of speech try to silence others who exercise that same right. These posters reveal the anxieties over what could happen when those of us oppressed by systems of whiteness start to pick at the cracks in its structure.

///

In minus 20 degree weather, I waited for the bus in my parka, an extra pair of mitts, and my winter boots. London winters are bone-chilling and the buses are never on time. After fifteen minutes, an older, white woman showed up. We exchanged a quick smile. The snow crunched underneath our boots as we waited.

"It's very cold!" I said.

"Oh, honey, you must not be used to this weather," she said sympathetically, looking me up and down. "I'm sure it must be hotter in the islands."

"Yeah, the islands would make a great trip right now!" I said. With reading week around the corner, I thought about all the warm places where I could make a last-minute escape.

She looked back, confused. "Yes, you must be used to that hot weather! You know, where you're from . . ." She paused at seeing my furrowed brow. ". . . In the islands."

"Uh, I was born here. In Canada."

"Oh, okay." She sounded reluctant to believe me. The bus arrived a minute later.

While working my first job on campus, helping first-years with their internet in residence, one of the cleaners, a woman with a European accent, saw me wiping away sweat on a hot day. "Why are you sweating like that? You must be used to this weather where you're from." And at a Tim Hortons in the winter of my final year, the cashier gave me the most pitiful glance.

"You poor dear, it must so hard adjusting to Canadian winters," she said, handing me my coffee.

"Well, no. I was born here," I replied.

"Oh, that's great. You speak English well."

Why is it so hard for some people to believe that anyone with beige or brown skin can be "from here?" Some of this ignorance can be attributed to the homogeneity of university towns. But things are changing: Southwestern Ontario, particularly London, has seen an 8 to 15 per cent shift in demographic over the last decade, with more immigrants moving to the city and students coming in from outside the region. This has brought with it a fear of people of colour, and an uptick in white nationalism and hate crimes. In 2010, London ranked fifth in Canadian metropolitan areas for police-reported hate crimes. Reported hate crimes in London increased by *over half* from 2016 to 2017, making it the largest rate in Southwestern Ontario.

There was a time when Black people considered London one of the country's more accepting cities. By the early 1850s, over 40,000 refugee slaves and free Blacks who came to Canada from the U.S. settled in Southern Ontario. London's geography made it an ideal home for refugee slaves who came through the Underground Railroad: while kidnappings of slaves were commonplace at border points like Windsor and Niagara Falls, London was far enough for safety.

London was a bustling little town that was home to some of the richest Black settlers in Ontario. They had more opportunity to make a living and own property in London than in larger cities like Toronto. But a man named Alfred T. Jones said that in London there was a "mean prejudice" that couldn't be found in the States. Several slave accounts corroborate this, including that of Frances Henderson, a man who said Black people were turned away from hotels. By the early 1860s, segregated schools were in the works, but a lack of funding halted the idea.

The Ku Klux Klan were active in London by 1872. That year the city welcomed a South Carolina Klansman who was fleeing U.S. police after murdering a Black man, and when he was finally captured, there was outcry among white Canadians, who viewed him as a hero. A decade later, a group of white hoodlums burned down the childhood home of a London-born Black man named Richard Berry Harrison, who was the son of fugitive slaves. It happened about two days after he and his family moved to Detroit. Harrison later became a renowned actor and was on the cover of *Time* magazine in 1935.

Today, London is home and rally territory to several far-right and white supremacist groups. Far- and alt-right protesters clash with counter-protesters in the city, and white pride marches take place on main streets, not far from Western. Hate speech and hate-promoting activity became so problematic that, in 2017, the City of London announced that the Managing Director of Parks and Recreation would be able to refuse or revoke permission for events on city grounds if they believed it promoted hatred or discrimination. Hate incidents in the city have been so shocking that they've made national headlines.

In 2011, during my second year, a man threw a banana peel on the ice while Wayne Simmonds of the Philadelphia Flyers was skating towards the goalie during the shootout of an NHL exhibition game at the John Labatt Centre. The man's lawyer said he was "oblivious to the racial connotations" and he only received a $200 fine. In February 2016, E.B. Smith—a Black actor from Cleveland who was playing Martin Luther King Jr. in a local production—said he had been the victim of racial slurs twice since arriving in London. Three months later, a Western University Ph.D. student from Iran was beaten outside the Covent Garden Market in downtown London. His attackers allegedly told him to go back to where he came from as they hit him. They were later charged with assault. The next month, a thirty-eight-year-old woman attacked a twenty-five-year-old Muslim woman, spitting on her and pulling at her hijab. The Muslim woman emerged with a black eye and chipped teeth, and the attacker was charged with assault.

In April 2017, Cody Perkin was charged with manslaughter and assault after brutally beating Vijay Bhatia, a London cab driver, to death. Video footage from witnesses caught Perkin telling Bhatia to "Go back to India," and uttering other slurs as he pummelled him. In 2018, Perkin was sentenced to four years, but with two years of time served counting towards his sentence, he will soon be out of jail. In December 2017, a Black family said they found "Nigger" written in the snow on their car and were considering moving out of London.

In July 2018, a thirty-nine-year-old London man was charged with assault, forcible confinement, and causing a disturbance after a viral video showed him blocking another man from leaving a grocery store. He called the man an illegal alien. Police initially let the attacker go with a warning, saying it was difficult to prove whether the incident was race-related or a hate crime, and didn't charge the man with assault until two weeks later, presumably only after public outcry.

During the 2018 municipal election, supporters said their signs for Arielle Kayabaga, a candidate running in Ward 13 and the first Black woman to be elected in London, were vandalized and urinated on several times. When Sudanese-born Mohamed Salih, London city councillor for Ward 3, was running back in 2014, two of his campaign signs were destroyed with fried chicken and watermelon. We have no hate crime laws, so criminal charges like assault, mischief, and damage to property are often used instead, as proving hate or bias is difficult.

With a rapidly changing landscape that is perceived to threaten white privilege, the "Go back to your country" rhetoric has become the attack of choice for the far right, white nationalists, and social conservatives. It's a phrase that exposes the fear of our diversifying country, of losing the benefits that come with maintaining the status quo. Its use can't be understated: it often accompanies threats or violence, and targets all people of colour, despite their nationality. It's also a political tactic amid a global wave of anti-immigration sentiment. In the U.S., it has been used by Donald Trump to throw immigrants into detention centres, to keep out migrants, and to dismiss any criticisms by people of colour over his administration. In July 2019, the "Go back to your country" discussion was renewed when Trump attacked four new Democratic members of Congress on Twitter—all women of colour; all U.S.-born except for Representative Ilhan Omar, who is a Somali refugee—and told them to go back to their country. Emboldened by his comment and his continued attacks on Omar, the crowd at his North Carolina rally days later chanted, "Send her back."

At its core, "Go back to your country" is the embodiment of the white rage—white fear—that has been responsible for many mass killings in schools, places of worship, public spaces, and workplaces. The Anti-Defamation League's 2017 report found that in the past decades white supremacists and right-wing extremists committed the majority of murders in the U.S.—more than double the number of the year before. Nearly every year, white supremacists commit the highest percentage of extremist-related murders—not refugees or immigrants.

Since I graduated in 2014, hate crimes in Canada have been increasing steadily, hitting an all-time high in 2017—nearly doubling from the year before. The majority of these crimes were race-based: Muslim, Jewish, and Black populations were the targets of most incidents. Experts like Dr. Barbara Perry have been documenting the rise of far-right extremism in the country for decades; she estimates that there are more than two hundred right-wing groups in Canada, and the number is only increasing. Despite years of these warnings, the Canadian Security Intelligence Service only recently began recognizing that right-wing extremist groups are a significant problem. In March 2019, Public Safety Canada announced it would be giving Perry and her team at the University of Ontario Institute of Technology $366,985 over three years to study right-wing extremism.

White rage is considered a legitimate, acceptable form of anger—one intended to maintain the integrity and purity of the country—so it is rarely viewed as threatening. White rage encourages and enacts violence against bodies of colour; yet when people of colour speak up against harm, they are told by society that they don't have a right to be angry. That there is nothing to be angry about, that they are dramatic and irrational. That they should stop complaining and go back where they came from. People of colour are not supposed to be angry about white rage, even when that rage seeks to hurt them. And as we ignore it, dismiss it, say it isn't that bad, it only grows worse.

///

With five suitcases full of food, cooking utensils, and clothes, my grandfather brought his family to Canada.

They arrived from Karachi on a cool, breezy day in April 1973. It was two years after the Canadian government announced its multiculturalism policy, and South Asian immigrants were coming to the country in droves. My family lived with my great-aunt, who had sponsored them, and within two weeks, my grandfather got a job bookkeeping at a nursing home run by a white couple, making $2.25 an hour. He and the white employees got the same salary; the Black workers got $2.00.

It was an easy decision to move to Canada. The country offered a place to raise a family and move up in society without fear of repercussions.

A few weeks after arriving in the country, my grandfather was on his way to work when a group of men in a car approached him and yelled, "Go back to your country, Paki!" My grandfather, the calmest person I know, picked up a rock and chased the car down the street. On the bus, walking to work, even in front of their house, the attacks were the same: *You Pakis, go back to your country.*

That didn't stop them from going out in public. They had family picnics at parks on red-and-white checkered tablecloths alongside white families. They went camping and watched the fireworks on Canada Day. In the summer, the whole extended family carpooled to Niagara Falls. My mother and uncle grew up like other teens, hanging out with their friends until late and listening to their idol Prince loudly in their rooms. The comments by strangers dwindled with time. So, it came as a surprise to my family when I told them that the same kind of derogatory comments, the ones that had pierced them so deeply many years ago, were aimed at me. My family rarely spoke about racism, or anything polarizing: politics, religion, injustice. They knew what it meant to be told to go back to their country—they had once been new immigrants to Canada—but I was born here, how could people say those things to me? How could that kind of hate exist after all these decades?

In my early twenties, as I started writing more about anti-Black racism and my work became visible, my relatives were surprised at the stories I covered. "Why do you write about them when you're one of us?" they asked. As if I'd been done a favour to have South Asian blood. As if being born Black were a curse.

I know they wanted to understand what I was going through, to understand how best to support me. But anti-Black racism, this unfamiliar type of injustice, was hard for them to comprehend, especially when they didn't see me as a Black woman.

My family was surprised to hear me refer to myself as Black. There was no simple way of explaining to my relatives that, regardless of how they saw me and how I had grown up, I was intrinsically tied to the things they didn't want to talk about, the things they didn't want to think could happen to me: police violence, discrimination, genetic health issues. I could never pass for a brown body like theirs, as much as they believed I could. I didn't share their skin colour or their features. People didn't care what family I was born into, if I was "mixed" or not—my body moved through the world as a Black woman, and that's how I was treated and perceived. That's who I was, despite also being South Asian; despite being multiracial.

They had always been extremely supportive of my decisions, no matter how rash. They let me figure out who I was on my own, and encouraged me to pursue the things I loved—reading, writing, going out with friends. When I applied to university, they supported my eventual decision to switch into an arts program, even though they wanted me to study something more sustainable like nursing or social work. Being my own person was always encouraged in my household, but referring to myself as Black in front of them seemed to make them question if they really knew me the way they thought they did.

I couldn't explain to them that unapologetically embracing my Black identity wasn't a sudden realization—it was survival. It gave me a sense of belonging in a city that made me an outsider; a way to both protect myself and make sense of these new experiences. It was empowering and magical, and I wasn't ashamed. To live somewhere like London, I needed to know who I was. Western was not like high school; I couldn't live in the in-between. There were no light skin and dark skin teams, no mixed-race camps. There was white and Black, and you were treated accordingly.

Resentfully, I closed myself off to my family, unwilling to share any more stories. If I couldn't even tell them about the slurs and microaggressions, how could I tell them about the close calls with violence? Or that I was depressed—that I was *scared* of everything and everyone? That I feared for my life every day, whether they believed it was rational or not?

Faced with their lack of understanding about how anti-Black racism affected my studies and my health, I found other ways of seeking encouragement. I enrolled in more race-related courses. I started reading the works of more Black scholars and feminists, feeling at home in their words; and I started documenting my experiences, which I could identify in the theories and stories of other writers.

It still wasn't enough to curb the loneliness, and food became a replacement for my emotions. After class, I'd go to the grocery store or pick up takeout from my favourite restaurant and then eat it all in one sitting. Instead of going out, I would go home and eat. Being painfully full distracted me from my racing thoughts.

Numerous, detailed studies have shown that racism is a chronic stressor, and experiencing anti-Black racism has serious mental and physical health effects. Experiencing discrimination or microaggressions every day—or simply living in fear of experiencing them—can cause enough stress to increase the risk of anxiety, depression, suicide or suicidal thoughts, common colds, cardiovascular disease, breast cancer, hypertension, and high blood pressure. These extensive studies into minority stress have been conducted in the U.S. and the U.K., but are harder to come by in Canada, even though Black Canadians have one of the worst health profiles in the country.

Black people are constantly at risk for developing health issues or having them worsen. Much has been written about how socio-economic discrimination affects Black Canadians in terms of employment, education, and housing, as well as the justice system. And the stress of experiencing racial discrimination on a daily basis also has a significant impact on the achievement of Black students, negatively affecting their success and causing them to drop out, fear going to school, and develop mental health issues.

I needed help carrying this heavy burden of racism, and I'd thought my family could alleviate some of it. We had experienced the same things in the same country, the same rejection, the same hopelessness. But there was a sea of distance between us.

/ / /

On a hot summer day when I was eight years old, my mom hit a bird with her car. She was shaking with dread as two of her co-workers pulled out the injured, screeching bird from the car grille and killed it. *A bad omen.*

I was aimlessly playing a Nickelodeon Flash game on the computer at my cousin's house, counting down the hours until my mom picked me up, when my great-uncle came in and told me my grandmother was in the hospital.

Scans showed a golf-ball sized tumour in her brain. CNS lymphoma. Six months to live. If she tried the experimental treatment—one year. She figured there was nothing to lose if it promised her more time with her family.

She beat the cancer. But when she started turning yellow, there wasn't a single nurse or doctor who thought to check for jaundice. The chemo had destroyed her liver. By the time they figured it out, nothing could be done.

My grandmother died at the end of March 2000. She did not get to see the melting snow make way for the bloom of purple tulips, her favourite. I was almost nine. Our house, my safe place, wasn't the same.

My thirty-one-year-old mother, who worked the early morning shift, had no time to make me elaborate lunches, just microwaved frozen meals that hardened by noon. She found other mothers who could watch me before school started, and take me to class. After school, she took me to the mall to eat—sometimes Taco Bell, other times our favourite Indian restaurant—denying the exhaustion etched on her face.

My mother stepped up as the matriarch of the house, taking on domestic chores for the first time and trying to make me and my grandfather Indian dishes with Shan spice mixes she got from the grocery store up the street, where my grandma had shopped. As the fumes of her ketchup-infused chana masala permeated the house, we ate in silence, and she watched, knowing that it wasn't my grandmother's cooking and none of us would get that ever again.

In the evenings, my grandfather helped me with my homework and took me to the movies. I looked forward to our Sundays together, when we swam at the community pool then went to Chapters, the bookstore. My grandfather would sit patiently at Starbucks for hours while I ran my fingers along the rows of book spines, desperately wanting to have my own book wedged among the others on the shelves.

I had always loved reading. As a child, my room overflowed with books that my grandmother read to me every night. I asked for more and more; I shoved them in my closet, rereading them and reorganizing them for fun. I refused to throw a single one out, even as they went on to fill two bookshelves in the basement and all the extra storage space in my room. My family encouraged my love of reading; an only child, books took me to an imaginary world where I could feel less alone.

It was hard adjusting to my new life without my grandmother, and books helped me escape our new reality. But once I finished my latest read, I felt overwhelmed by loneliness again, ripped from my temporary, colourful cocoon. So I started to think about ways that I could keep the stories going, ploys to stay in my protective bubble: I started writing.

While my Grade 4 teacher taught us math, I wrote a children's picture book about grief. While my Grade 7 teacher taught us factually incorrect, homophobic sex-ed from our *Fully Alive* textbook, I was writing scandalous Good Charlotte and Mest fan fiction that resembled a high school TV drama. I continued to pen fan fic until I turned fifteen, when I traded being an emo loner for friends and a social life. By Grade 11, I started writing op-eds for the school newspaper, which soon earned me my own column. I wrote throughout study period and lunch, in my evenings after homework, and at night before bed. That year, I won a short story contest for young writers.

My grandfather took notice of my endless notebooks and large stash of pens. Each morning, just as he'd done as a child in Karachi, he woke up early to read the newspaper. Then he'd leave me clippings from the Books section—profiles and reviews of South Asian authors—on the living room table so I could read them on the way to school. "This fellow is Pakistani," he'd say, beaming with pride as he traced his finger over the page. His finger smudged the ink like when he used to help me with my homework. *See, you can do it too.*

I'd read the article over and over, willing myself to feel inspired. But I couldn't identify with their success. Instead, I saved the clippings and stored them in a box, hoping one day to look back and feel what I wasn't able to then.

My grandfather continued to save me newspaper clippings, even after I graduated high school and moved to London, even after I began writing more about what it meant to be a Black woman on campus. On the weekends I came home to visit, he'd leave them on the table—more successful South Asian authors, more wins for our people. "This woman won an award for her book," he'd say, pointing at her high-resolution headshot. *See, you can do it too.*

When I started my Master of Journalism at Ryerson University in Toronto, the clippings included stories by South Asian journalists in addition to authors. By this time I was writing my own stories about anti-Black racism and reporting on issues affecting Black communities. My grandfather printed them out and kept them for his own collection, to share with people he knew. Still, he wanted to know if I planned on writing stories like the ones that brown journalists covered. "How come you don't write about South Asian culture? It's your culture too."

It was never accusatory, and yet I felt put on the spot. Until that moment, I hadn't given it much thought, and with good reason. It had been the culture I was raised in, but the way I navigated the world—the issues that people who looked like me were dealing with—was very different than what I was born into. I couldn't admit that although I was born and raised in that culture—and belonged to it—I would never identify with it the way the rest of my family were able to.

That year, on a clifftop restaurant while vacationing in Sorrento, Italy, I had my first conversation about my identity with my grandfather. Over a Margherita pizza, I told him I was grateful for never having been treated differently, but the avoidance of discussing my identity had created a disconnect in the way that they understood my experiences. I described the years of struggling in high school, then at Western, and then being one of the few journalists of colour in the industry.

I was unsure if I had ruined our relationship and our vacation. "Is it because you're half Black?" he asked. It was the first time he ever said it—*Black*—the first acknowledgement in twenty-three years. He recalled moments of racism throughout my childhood, when he didn't think I was old enough to understand what was happening. We talked about his own trouble fitting in at school as a young, poor boy; his struggles in coming to Canada from Pakistan with nothing but hope; the sacrifices he and my grandmother had made in order to raise his family and keep a roof over our heads. The pain of those hateful comments as they tried to build a life here. The purpose of the clippings was to remind me of where I came from. And that, like him, like those authors, I could do whatever I aspired to.

This moment forged a path for my family to become my fiercest advocates. When I come home on the weekends now, newspaper clippings about books by Black authors greet me on the table. I see myself in these writers; their successes fuel my own. Over lunch, my grandfather and I catch up to talk about what I'm writing, and discuss the latest news stories to do with discrimination. My mother and I have long, engaging conversations about race and she listens instead of dismissing me. There are no longer silences or excuses. Instead there are furrowed brows and anger—for me, that I live in a world that they now see will not shield me from a problem they thought was long over.

It took some time, but my eagerness to invite them into my world and their willingness to listen has put us in a place where I feel supported talking to them about what I experience. And though there's still a part of my mother that doesn't get my decision to identify as Black, she is starting to understand that perhaps people don't see me the way she does—that *I* don't see me the way she does.

My family is learning that the best way to support me is not to deny our stark differences but to embrace them. It's about believing that I can experience anti-Black racism and still be their Pakistani child. It's about actively learning how race informs who we are and how we see the world, including in our own families. It's about breaking down the parental power dynamic and being willing to learn from their child. This is allyship. This is love.

It is not a betrayal to see and experience the world differently from the rest of your family, and it is not the responsibility of any multiracial child to have to explain how they identify. Multiracial bodies are heavily politicized sites of learning and possibility. We are uncomfortable conversations, and messy identity politics. Our blood is a mix of contradictions: love and hate, oppressed and oppressor, and pain and healing.

///

We were about to start the hora, and David had just told me that a guy had made a comment to him about the nigger at the party.

I was the only Black person at Krista's wedding. As we got ready to dance, the wannabe white supremacist who had just called me a nigger stood beside me. His hand reached out for mine, clammy palm outstretched, the last two people to connect the circle. I looked at him: hairy, sweat all over his face and in the armpits of his dress shirt, hair matted to his wrinkled forehead, his tinted bottlecap glasses slightly foggy. And because I didn't want to make a scene among the good white folk, I put my hand in his.

Krista had warned me that he would be at the wedding. Everyone knew about his extracurricular activities on white supremacist and neo-Nazi forums, and how he frequently spoke about his disgust for Black people, Jews, and women—despite the fact that he was Arab. The irony was not lost on me.

Krista and I had met in second year, and now, as we were going into fourth year, we had become good friends. This made my decision over whether to attend her wedding even more difficult. For months I wondered whether I should retract my RSVP. Not for my safety—I had other friends who would be attending—but rather in protest. But I didn't want to make Krista and her husband choose; I worried that if I asked, they'd pick him.

I put on my best poker face during the ceremony and the reception. I drank scotch and chatted with my friends, occasionally watching him from the corner of my eye. We avoided each other all night.

After dinner, a group of us were sitting outside when David, my friend's boyfriend, told me about the comment. He had told the white supremacist that he wasn't okay with him talking about me like that. The guy was not a very good white supremacist— he tried to backpedal his comments.

As David told the story, I instinctively felt my wrist flex. *Flat palm. Maximum damage.*

The rest of the group thanked David. It was such a nice, cool thing to stand up for me, they told him. For years afterwards, at get-togethers with Krista, her husband, and their friends, I had to hear about how a white man had come to my rescue. Her husband eventually ended his friendship with the white supremacist, but the story lived on. I don't think anyone ever asked me how I felt about it, or questioned why a man like that was there in the first place. Nobody thought about the impact of having to relive this moment at every get-together, where it was retold for entertainment. I was the voiceless victim saved by a white man—reassurance to themselves that not all white people were bad, that they could be allies.

But I was not defenceless, and nor had I ever been. I wasn't hurt about being called a nigger—especially by some guy who was too much of a coward to say it to my face. I had options: I could have gone back into the reception hall and confronted him. I could've ignored it because he wasn't worth a conversation. I could've taken my flattened palm and driven it sharply up his nose—I knew how.

That night, after the wedding, I thought about Angela. She and my mother had had a falling out when I was still a kid, and at that age it didn't occur to me to ask for her number to keep in touch. For years, I've wanted to call her and thank her for doing what my own family wasn't able to.

Angela was the only one to tell me the truth: I was a Black girl. This world didn't give two shits what family I grew up in, how Black I was, how mixed I was. She was preparing me for the reality that having this skin meant I had to be informed and always ready to fight for myself. I didn't need sugar-coating or denial. I needed someone to see me the way my family couldn't.

As a child, I'd spent so much time with Angela, sitting quietly on the milk crates in her garage, listening to her and my mom tell their profanity-laced stories while I drank chocolate milk. She knew I could never actually inflict the kind of assault she'd taught me, but that wasn't the point. The palm strike wasn't to show me how to break someone's nose; it was to get me ready for the inevitable day that I was angry and fed up, and caught off guard by that word. *Nigger*. In a world that would often leave me feeling out of control, it gave me permission to harness that fury and anger. To have the option for revenge and decide not to use it—that was more potent than their words. That was power. And if I were ever in danger—well, at least I knew how to defend myself.

To live our lives unashamedly and openly, we always risk pain—at our own hands, at the hands of our families, at the hands of a stranger. Angela knew that, and she knew I'd learn that too. She taught me that I had permission to feel that pain and to react to it if I needed to; but most of all, that it would be an inevitable part of my life. Only I could decide if it would consume me.

I hope one day we meet again.

The Token Partier

WHAT TO EXPECT: Paranoid that people are pointing, laughing, and talking about you? They are. Drunk people will approach you just to say that you're the first Black person they've ever spoken to (you might also be the best-dressed, best-smelling, best-looking—the list goes on). You'll be approached by some idiot who will eye you like a Swiss Chalet quarter-chicken dinner and say, like a boy who has just discovered the joys of masturbation, that he's never danced with a Black girl before. Will you be his first? If you're a guy, you may get searched or denied entry or service at the bar because of your "urban wear." This is a lie—there are a hundred Post Malones and Machine Gun Kellys partying it up inside right now and we all know it.

HOW TO DEAL WITH IT: The good news is that Black people have the upper hand in these spaces. When you combine us with the dark ambiance and hip-hop music, people think we're extra scary. Give them *the look* (you know which one). This will make any guy back off, and the girl who body-slammed you on her way through the crowd with her friends will apologize like she's begging for her life.

visible
bruises

Joshua,

The halls of our high school were buzzing with frantic, excited whispers, not at all the appropriate tone for what had just happened that weekend.

I texted you as soon as I heard about it. We both loved Chris Brown. We loved him and Rihanna as a couple even more. But now, just before the Grammys, they had gotten into an argument in a car. He had been caught in a lie again, and she'd grilled him for the truth. As they argued, his eyes became dark—there was no soul. He started to hit her, punch her, over and over. She waited for it to stop. Months later, she'd say that their relationship was tumultuous, obsessive, co-dependent. Brown was charged with assault, and photos of Rihanna's battered face became a permanent fixture on the internet.

During school, the sounds of Brown's music, which filled the halls on LG phones and on CD players as kids rehearsed their after-school dances, were now replaced by angry conversations about Rihanna. She had ruined the life of their beloved, attractive American superstar. *She was mouthy. She was sassy. She was probably bitching at him. She wanted attention. She should've let it go.*

We were both sixteen. It was the first time I had seen violence against a woman. Not you—growing up, you saw it often in your own home. I couldn't understand how someone could do that to the person they loved. I couldn't understand you, making jokes about it already. But the students around me were convinced Rihanna was no victim; their list of reasons growing longer and more outrageous. *She was probably cheating too. She started it. She did it to herself.* I shamefully wondered if, in the collective blame, there could be some truth.

"She must have done something to deserve it," you said as we walked to Chemistry class, a month before you became my first boyfriend, my first love. "I'd probably do the same."

And you would, when your hand curled into a fist against my jaw two years later.

/ / /

We had crossed paths often over the years. You were the class clown, not necessarily popular—at least not with the white kids who dominated the social food chain—but your other Asian friends thought you were cool. I was a keener, a straight-A student and president of the youth leadership group, and I desperately wanted a thrill. You looked at me and smirked as I passed by you in the halls. When you shouted out, "Eternity, you're gonna live forever," I rolled my eyes and kept on walking, but really, I liked it.

In class, you helped me with formulas. When I got impatient, you let me copy your answers. In return, I edited your essays. I thought you were equally badass and nerdy, both overly confident and terribly insecure. I was intrigued, and I asked you to hang out. Tuesdays became the day we took the bus to the beach and smoked the cigarettes I never knew how you got. In between puffs, you asked me to be your girlfriend. I said yes. You were the first boy I ever kissed.

You were patient and gentle as I navigated this new romantic territory. You'd already had girlfriends; I was scared you would compare us. After school, we'd sit under the highway overpass and listen to the whooshing of cars above us; you kissed the back of my hand when it was clasped in yours. On the weekends, you'd take the bus to meet me at the mall, so we could take photos in the booth by the Yogen Früz and then see a movie. You were embarrassed you only had enough money to cover your ticket, not your popcorn. Afterwards, we'd hang out at my house watching TV and eating pizza. You made me laugh, and you liked the parts about me that had once been the reason I roamed the halls alone. It wasn't long before we exchanged *I love you*s.

How could you hold my hand and then later slide yours up my kilt as I pushed it away? How could you tell me you were happy we were waiting, and in the same breath throw your weight on me until I was immobilized, your hands clumsily yet forcefully trying to unzip my pants?

These things disturbed me, yet I told myself you were just being a typical teenage boy.

You didn't act like this during my first time. This time, I wanted you. You asked me several times if I was sure—you were concerned, loving. I had just turned seventeen.

When it was over, we got dressed and went outside. You pulled out your phone to record me. "I want to immortalize this moment," you said as I spun in circles with my umbrella, laughing. The afternoon sun warmed my body, surrounding me like a protective mother. Meanwhile, the rain dripped heavily like tears from the sky.

///

That summer, just before Grade 12, was a clash of sunny, humid days and aggressive rainfall. You and I joked that Lucifer was fighting with his wife. We searched for other interpretations on the desktop computer in my basement: *The devil is angry that God created a beautiful day, so he brutally beats his wife. The rain is her tears.*

By now, my kilt was well above the school's knee-length requirement, and I was wearing skin-tight trousers from the mall instead of the baggy ones from the uniform store. I ditched the glasses and invested in contacts, along with a full face of makeup. I no longer wore basic underwire bras from Walmart, opting for the padded sequined collection from La Senza. The edge of womanhood was thrilling, and at lunchtime Taz and I walked along the main roads smoking Superslims, our kilts swinging as male Toronto Catholic District School Board employees looked out the windows of their burgundy vans and honked.

From my baby fat, which I had struggled with for years, the curves of a woman's body had emerged. I became more con-fident in my shapely legs and flat stomach, and the ways I could show them off like the girls in teen magazines. I wore short shorts, miniskirts, and sundresses. On the bus to the mall, you pinched my leg under my Daisy Dukes. "That's your punishment for wearing those," you said. "No guy wants his girl showing off her body for other men."

But it wasn't for men; it was for me. When the red chaos of womanhood made its home in my body at only nine, it launched eight years of bullying. To the other kids, I had changed. I now had an adult body—abnormal, unrelatable. No one wanted to be marked by the girl with the period, who was developing much faster than the others. As puberty moved rapidly through my body, I got taller and fuller.

I wanted to be friends with the other girls, but their disgust over my natural bodily functions had shifted into a desire to constantly humiliate me. They kicked and slapped and teased me. When I told my teachers, they accused me of lying—these girls and their small bodies were so fragile. How dare I make up lies?

My grandmother's death had shaken up our household. I was fragile, and in my grief, I didn't know how to defend myself. My mother, angered by the slow staff response, spent every morning before and every afternoon after work in the principal's office, cussing him and his staff out, demanding that something be done, that they believe me. And when that didn't work, she would wait with me in the parking lot until the morning bell rang, her eyes on my bullies as she played Beenie Man and Elephant Man so loud that the car would shake and concerned white parents would stare. She'd light her Du Maurier and inhale, then turn to me, her nose and labret studs shimmering in the sun, and say, "If anybody fucks with you, you fuck them up. And when you get sent to the principal's office, you tell them that your mother told you to fucking do it, and if they have a problem, they can fucking call me. Don't forget this." And then she'd send me off with my big-ass backpack and the two neatly packed pepperoni Hot Pockets that she had over-microwaved.

The next time I got in trouble for defending myself, I told my teacher, as instructed, what my mother told me. Thinking I was bluffing, she called my mom. The teacher returned pale-faced and teary-eyed, and told me to go play.

That was so long ago. But now *you* were fucking with me—with my growth, my glow-up. Why did you want to suppress what was blossoming within me? I told you to mind your business, channelling the sass and ferocity I had seen my mother unleash on men who told her what do to. "The more you complain, the shorter my clothes will get," I snapped.

A boy had never even taken an interest in me before you, and your aggressive jealousy was as flattering as it was concerning. The slightest male attention sent you into a rage. In public, guys passed by me, stealing a glance, and you'd yank me to your chest and kiss me hard on the mouth while looking them in the eye. You'd grab my ass so hard it stung. "What the fuck are you looking at?" you'd yell. "This is mine."

Everything I knew about teenage boys was from high-school television dramas: *Gossip Girl, The O.C., One Tree Hill.* Boys were inherently sexually aggressive and jealous, and you dealt with it because you were lucky to be someone's girlfriend. That's where I also learned about love. There was no division between love and rage, between pain and passion—those were signs that you were loved deeply. I was lucky enough to be chosen by you, to be loved so fiercely by you, and I equated your control with love and devotion, despite my gut warning me that this was not what love should feel like. I continued to call it love, even when you demanded I stop hanging out with my girlfriends because you thought they were too feminist and headstrong. Even when you sulked when I spent the day with my mother and not you. Even when you wanted me to delete any male Facebook friend who liked my posts. Even when you told me I wasn't as smart or likeable as you.

I felt bad for thinking about breaking up with you. You had lost your friends when you defended me against their racist comments—the same friends who rapped in the halls and wore urban wear and styled their hair in cornrows—friends who were fine with Black culture as long as it wasn't on Black people. And your mother was barely talking to you now. How many times did you hurt me by telling me what your mother said: that I was ugly, that I wasn't welcome at her house? That Black girls were dirty, that I would use my sexuality to corrupt you? Do you ever think about the irony of that statement? Like your friends, you appropriated Black culture, and like your mother your obsessive comments about my skin colour and our inter-racial relationship were ignorant. I broke up with you once, at the end of summer, five months into our relationship. Ignoring my instinct had become so overwhelming that I blurted it out while we were watching TV. It lasted seventy-two hours. Then I took you back, worried my decision was premature, afraid of seeing you in the hallways.

Like me, you never planned on going to university or college. We both had working mothers; we wanted to replicate their lives, not realizing they had broken their backs to provide for us—that they wanted more for us than what they'd had. I decided to go.

The countdown to early-acceptance letters sparked an urgent desperation in you. All you talked about were the things I didn't want: marriage, children, living together. All I talked about was the new life I was looking forward to. You wanted me to stay. You reminded me every time you tampered with our protection or lied about not having condoms.

I wanted to end our relationship and enjoy the last few months with my friends and my family, but our lives felt so fused by our own imposed teenage standards. People knew us as a couple now; it had taken so long for the gossip to die down about the unlikely interracial pairing. When we weren't together they asked where you were. We shared a locker and took the same classes. I wondered what you would tell people if we broke up—would you reveal my secrets? Tell them that I was easy and gave it up too soon? Would you call me that word you toyed with when my clothes were too short—*slut*?

You had no one, and I was your everything. That was something I made up for by always being there for you and your needs, despite never being there for my own.

That only made me resentful and combative. I was angry at you for your dependency. I was angry at myself for enabling it. After school, we fought on the phone about your control over me and my refusal to be controlled. The next morning you came to school, your knuckles crusted over with dried blood from punching holes in your bedroom wall.

The day before I moved to London, you and I sat on a grassy hill at a park near my house. I had already decided that I would end our relationship when I got to university. You gently took my hand in yours. "Will you marry me?" you asked.

I searched your face, hoping it would crack into the smile you made when you were pranking me. "Are you serious? You don't even have a ring," I told you, rolling my eyes.

"I know, but I just want to claim you, so you're mine." You spoke softly, which you did when you were asking for something you knew you shouldn't.

"Joshua, we've talked about this so many times." I wanted to choose my words carefully. "I just . . . I need to experience other things."

"You mean you want to fuck other guys," you spat angrily, your voice now a low growl.

In the charged silence, you lifted the same hand that had just held mine up to your face, clenching it into a fist. Remains of crusted blood had made a home in your pale flesh.

"Look at this," you said, examining the scarred, bloody knuckles like precious stones. "One punch and I could kill you."

///

The morning after moving into my dorm room in Medway-Sydenham, I woke up to a flurry of your messages. *I can't believe you're gone. Come back, please. I hate you. Let's have a baby. I want to be with you forever. I wanna kill people, especially myself.* On the phone, you alternated between crying and screaming at me, for leaving you and ruining your life. I spent most of frosh week huddled in the corner of my room, listening to the muffled sound of bass and people partying in the hall—where I wanted to be—apologizing to you. I couldn't end it like this when you needed me.

On the last day of frosh week, when you finally realized no amount of messages would make me come home, you conceded. "I've been a jerk. Go have fun tonight, you deserve it," you said. It was the most rational you'd sounded in a long time. Taz and I cracked open the bottle of Smirnoff vodka we'd gotten an older first-year to buy for us. I didn't know how to measure liquor, and I drank a whole red Solo cup full. The intoxication was warm and fuzzy.

Taz and I made our way to University College Hill, pushing through the blur of over a thousand people in glow-in-the-dark necklaces, purple shirts, bandanas, and sunglasses. Faces and bodies painted in purple and white were moving against one another, dancing, tripping, and falling everywhere as music pounded from the stage, booming like it was coming from the sky. For once, I wasn't thinking about you.

I don't know how I got into that giant bouncy castle that night, but I do remember worrying that the security guards would kick me out. Instead they laughed and helped me up. I don't how I started talking to a guy there, but I know I pushed him away several times before letting him kiss me. I wanted to feel the weightlessness of not having responsibilities waiting for me in the form of threatening messages and voicemails. And I kissed him back—the easy way out of my shackles.

The sobering jolt of reality made me pull away. I ran all the way back to my dorm, sobbing, spitting out the taste of him. He was unfamiliar; I missed you now. I called you, crying. "What did you do?" You already knew. I begged you to forgive me, unable to stand being the villain. You were gone with a click.

The next morning, you called me back. "So, I've given it some thought, and I want us to work this out because I love you." Your voice was flat and emotionless.

My relief was short-lived. I wanted you to take me back, scared that what I had done had marked me as an unlovable whore. But the moment you hung up, the gradient of dread became steeper. I gave up my out. Now that you had taken me back, I owed it to you to stay.

A week after the kiss, I took the Greyhound bus to the mall to see you. You were waiting at the bottom of the steep escalator, your face expressionless. As I got off the last step, I put out my arms to hug you, and gasped as a sharp sting spread across the back of my leg. I looked at you, but your eyes were dead. "That's what you get for what you did," you said before giving me a tight smile, flexing the hand you'd just slapped me with, and then you walked off without me.

It took me a long time to come to terms with why I didn't leave you right then—or before that. The red flags piled up, one after the other, but I didn't believe any of it was violence. Violence seemed like something complete, unfragmented. The pieces—sometimes subtle, other times more obvious—made it hard to form a complete picture. How could you be so controlling but make me feel so loved? How could you use your hand to trace my lips with your fingers, then use it so forcefully against my skin? It was these grey areas that confused me—the bad with the good, the discomfort with the comforting. In high school, as the president of the leadership group, I taught the younger girls about dating violence. I ran through the red flags with them, I taught them how to spot guys like you. I knew better than to stay with you.

But I wasn't innocent either. I was flighty, cold, moody, and mean. I knew your limits and I ploughed through them to get a reaction. I held powerful grudges, much stronger than your gentle attempts to talk through our issues. I had my own problematic definitions of masculinity, chastising your emotion as weakness. I provoked you just to see how upset you could get.

You'd roughed me up play-fighting; I'd found it to be an immature assertion of masculinity. But this moment was deliberate. You played it off like a playful smack that accidentally went too far, but the deadness—the *darkness*—in your eyes was something I had never seen before. Yet I wasn't surprised at all. You had so much rage inside you, so much insecurity, a hell of a lot to prove—it was inevitable that you would explode. By then I was sure I'd be long gone.

///

Written in red at the top of my essay was a scribbled note that I could do better. I knew I could, and I knew I couldn't right now, so I shoved it in the bottom of my backpack, pretending not to see my favourite TA watching me, concerned.

My grades had slipped since you started leaving me messages again. There was a lull after that day at the mall—you got a job in construction and were making new friends, and I finally got to enjoy being a student. I went to all my classes and caught up with my friends in residence. It was nice to clutch a map of the campus instead of my phone. But that didn't last long.

I was at the library and you called four times. "What are you doing?" you asked me.

"I'm studying for my test. Is something wrong?" I said.

"No." You sounded annoyed. "I just want to know who you're with."

You did this every day at different times—as I went to class, as I worked on assignments, as I spent evenings unwinding with the rest of the floor in the common room. "Who are you with? Are you alone? Get on video chat to show me." You'd demand a full scan of the room. You thought I wouldn't notice that you were trying to catch me cheating. But you also forgot to mark my emails and Facebook messages back as unread when you hacked into my accounts to compile the information of everyone I knew. Before bed, you'd call on video chat again. "I need to make sure you're alone." This clouded my vision and made my heart race, and then I'd yell at you and we'd fight into the early morning. Taz became so used to it that she'd wear headphones to sleep when we spoke. I'd wake up the next afternoon to texts from a friend asking if I was coming to our morning class, along with a dozen erratic ramblings from you: you were sorry for being controlling; you knew I wanted to leave but you couldn't let me go. You loved me and wanted me to be happy, even if it was without you. You couldn't live without me. You didn't want me to live without you. You wanted to do to me what Chris Brown did to Rihanna.

The night I tried to break up with you, I remember you saying you were walking down to the train station to jump. I don't know if you actually went, but you were yelling and crying, "I will fucking kill myself if you leave me, and it will be your fault." I cried so hard in the girls' washroom that I had a panic attack. "Tell me you won't leave, ever, or I'll do it right now," you repeated, over and over.

"I promise," I gasped, clutching my chest for air. "I promise, I promise. I promise."

I wanted to get us both help, but I didn't know where to go on campus. I had only been in this new environment for a few weeks, I couldn't even remember the buildings that housed my classes. During appointments at the OB/GYN's office, I laid on the exam table, staring at the foot stirrups covered by pieces of cloth that said "Abused? You can talk to me." I almost considered saying something but the thought of being exposed from the waist down, legs spread wide, as I caught the poor doctor off guard with my confession—they probably didn't even put those cloths there—made me laugh. I wouldn't have minded talking to a professional, but they weren't easy to find. I could barely figure out what services were available on campus and where to look. There were some posters about sexual assault, and support services for survivors; I hadn't recognized that part of our relationship yet. I wanted to call your mom while you were at work, but I didn't think she would believe me. And I didn't want to worry my own mother. She always joked that I had redeemed her: I had done well in school. I was trustworthy. She never had to deal with me getting into trouble the way she had. I couldn't tell her just how dark our relationship had become. I couldn't bring myself to shatter the illusion she had about her only child. Instead, I asked Taz and another friend from residence for advice.

They both rolled their eyes and said you were just being stupid. "He's Asian, he can't do anything to you," Taz said.

"Girl, just beat his ass," the other friend said. "You're Black."

You were just being immature, nothing that I couldn't handle, they suggested. My friends believed I could fend off abuse simply because I was a Black woman. I was supposed to be angry, defensive, indestructible, physically and emotionally unbreakable. By virtue of our respective races and the stereotypes that followed, it was impossible for them to believe that I was in as much danger as I claimed. The stereotype of the effeminate Asian man—submissive, passive, non-threatening—meant that, in their minds, you were incapable of such abuse. Your presumed passivity was no match for my presumed aggression. I resolved that maybe things weren't as bad as I thought. Maybe all I needed was to defend myself better, to put you in your place and make you afraid of me.

But you were already afraid of me, and who I was becoming without you.

///

When you showed up to my dorm on Halloween, it didn't bother you that I didn't kiss you hello. It didn't bother you to know how much I hated you.

We were barely speaking, unless you called me—even those conversations turned into a screaming match. I wanted you out of my life, and you threatened to end yours when I told you. I didn't want you coming up for my first Halloween weekend at Western—I had been looking forward to spending it with my friends. You dropped so many hints about showing up either way that the best way to avoid more drama was just to invite you.

You enthusiastically poured Taz and me drinks as we got ready. "I want you to have fun tonight. Pretend I'm not here," you said, handing me another drink.

I took it, suspicious about your encouragement. "Can you stop making these drinks so strong? They're disgusting," I snapped. You ignored my annoyance and diluted the drink with pop, smiling.

"Anything you want."

We went to a party down the hall. I was already slipping in and out of consciousness. All I could hear was one loud, jumbled conversation over the bass of the music. My eyes felt swollen, and I couldn't lift my head to look up at you to tell you to stop pushing the cup to my lips. I remember trying to move away, and alcohol spilling down my shirt. People came by to take pictures as I slumped over, saying that they hadn't seen me like this before. Your voice was so sober as you explained that you hadn't either.

Even though the room was spinning, it was you who made my stomach tighten. You pulled my arm, your breath hot and prickly in my ear. "Let's go back to your room. I want to be alone." I tried to move away from you. I told you to go back on your own. But I was too drunk to keep fighting you.

I remember loudly yelling "I'll be back!" into the crowded room, an instinct—even in my inebriated state—to make sure someone heard me in case I didn't return.

I walked slowly behind you. Had I had so much to drink that I was making myself paranoid? How could I be this unnerved about being alone with you?

We got into the room and you shut the door behind us. I leaned against it, the cold hanging mirror pressing against my exposed lower back, giving me a sobering jolt. You set the key down on my desk, your back facing me.

"Can we go back and see my friends?" I wanted to sound commanding so you'd be too afraid to do whatever you were about to do. Instead, my voice came out hoarse and small.

"No." Yours was stern. You still hadn't turned around. Outside, the other first-years were drunkenly yelling and laughing in the courtyard. I wished I was out there with them. I looked at the fuchsia digital clock on the ledge under the window: it was just after 10 p.m. The room was quiet except for the clinking of your Batman belt buckle that I had bought you for Christmas. I wanted the mirror to suck me up and make me disappear.

When you finally turned around, your face was pale and expressionless. Your jaw was clenched, and your eyes were cold and dead like I had seen once before. I don't remember how I got from standing against the door to being on the floor in front of it. I counted the seconds before the darkness came for me, and just before it took over, I forced my heavy head up to look in the mirror and see this ugly reflection, this unspeakable reality. I kept my eyes on myself until I had no choice but to surrender.

I didn't know what to call what you did to me. You were my boyfriend, not a stranger at a frat party. I didn't say yes or no; I was blacked out. I didn't want your drinks, but I took them anyway. And despite being unsure of what happened, I felt violated by you. That word, *rape*, danced on the tip of my tongue but it did not leave my mouth. It tingled there as you packed your bag, and I closed my lips and swallowed it, and you went home.

I didn't know what you did to me, and yet I knew what you did to me. I knew it was bad enough that I would never forget it, and I knew it was bad enough that I couldn't be with you anymore.

Moving away, talking back, fighting, trying to love each other harder—it had made everything worse. I wanted so many things—a new life, new friends, new experiences—but our relationship had kept me from so much of it. It made me stressed, frightened, and hopeless. This wasn't love, it couldn't be.

I could now admit what this relationship was: abusive. And, now that I could see it, there was nothing left to lose.

///

Do you remember how we broke up? It happened so quickly, that descent into chaos. It started with me screaming at you at the top of my lungs when you asked me who I was with, then telling you we were breaking up for good. It ended with you taking a Greyhound bus to London at 3 a.m., hopping a twelve-foot spiked fence, and standing above my bed with a rusty hammer an inch from my face. I managed to calm you down and make you understand that we were done, and somehow you accepted it and went home.

At first, I felt peace without you. I caught up in class, my 60s back up to 80s. I left my phone in my room while I hung out with the other people on my floor. I slept well. They put your photo up by security, and campus police was notified not to let you on the property. But soon, I was thinking about you again. I blamed myself for how our relationship ended. I knew I didn't miss you; I missed the idea of who you could be, the lost opportunities for us to be healthy and functional. I romanticized you and your actions. I craved your comfort and familiarity. You knew all my secrets, my bad habits, my fears, my faults. Despite your control over my body, the way you isolated me from my friends, how you forced yourself on me—classic signs of an abuser—I needed you. Before I moved away, it was your shirt I'd soaked with my homesick tears. I no longer loved you, yet the pain of never speaking to you again, and the fear that I had sealed my fate of being alone forever, made it feel as if I'd never be able to rebuild a life without you.

I don't remember when we started talking again, but I know I reached out first. I blocked this part out of my mind, the month leading up to the climax of our volatile relationship, the steep climb towards the peak of violence. I made it very clear we were just friends, that we should date other people. You agreed. We were spending just as much time together as before, but we were worse now. I purposely provoked your anger, and you flipped tables in public and yelled at me until I was backed into a corner. I told you I hated you. You told me you did too, but that you still loved me. We were co-dependent, destructive, explosive.

I was so ashamed by this darkness within both of us. I came home to break our cycle for good. I asked you to come over. I wanted to be proud of myself for ending this, and I thought you'd be proud of me too. But when I went into the kitchen, you unlocked my phone and saw a text I had sent to another guy. All the colour in your face drained away except for your bloodshot eyes. Sweat beaded on your upper lip. You were yelling—your voice was hoarse—something about showing everyone what a slut I was, but I couldn't hear the rest. The room swelled with the anticipation of having to endure something terrible. "I will kill you," you promised, moving closer. I knew it was inescapable when I looked in your eyes, wide and bulging, and couldn't reach you.

When it was over, that moment of extreme violence I'd always known would come, you calmly dialled 911, handed me the phone, and ran. My mother and her boyfriend showed up just after the police, and yet they began asking *him* questions, the Black man. When you returned from around the corner, sweaty, guilty, the officers were speechless even after you confessed, as if someone like you wasn't capable of such violence.

Joshua, I have written you many letters since that day. These handwritten letters, spanning several pages, are tear-stained and fading in a box of our memories. I have a dozen more on old computers. None of them have been sent. I wrote you when I left school for two weeks right before exams because I was scared that you'd show up at my dorm again. I wrote you after you posted a photo of you and your new girlfriend on Facebook on the day that would have been our anniversary. I wrote you when I woke up screaming, drenched in sweat from nightmares. I wrote you when I moved back home after first year and couldn't leave the house all summer. I wrote you when my anxiety was so bad I couldn't drive the car I used to drive you to school in. I wrote you when my depression made me not want to live, and my all-consuming anger and grief drowned everyone around me. I wrote you because we were just teenagers with terrible notions of what love was. I wrote you because you were the last link to my old life as I tried to build a new one.

At some point in each letter, I shamefully ask you the same question: "Do you think I deserved it?"

Do you think I deserved it? Do you think I deserved it? Do you think I deserved it?

Did I think I deserved it?

This is my last letter to you. The rest are to myself.

///

"You need to call the arresting officer immediately and file more charges." The woman on the phone sounded concerned. I had finally found a domestic assault hotline for women of colour. The woman I spoke to confirmed the red flags in my relationship with Joshua: stalking, harassment, sexual assault.

The compassion of this stranger validated the severity of my relationship, and I needed it. My friends didn't understand. I had always been functional, even through bouts of anxiety or sadness. But that was working against me now. Everyone around me was desperate to believe that I was not in pieces. They didn't know how to be around me or what to say, especially since they all knew and liked Joshua.

I left a voicemail for the officer that day, and he got back to me later in the week. "I'd like to file other charges—"

"Look, it doesn't matter whether you file additional charges because the court will see it's a first-time offence and drop it anyway," he said nonchalantly. "You could speak to Victim Services if you need support."

There's a deeply held belief that Black women *can't* be abused and won't tolerate it. Since slavery, Black women have been viewed as strong, animalistic, and unwomanly—able to fend for themselves, to withstand physical and mental hardship.

Studies on intimate partner violence have found that racial bias affects the way Black female victims are treated by law enforcement, society, and their own communities, because they don't adhere to the myth of the "perfect victim." While Black women are significantly more likely to experience intimate partner violence and inter-partner homicide than women from any other demographic, and are four times more likely to die at the hands of a current partner, they are also more likely to be arrested or jailed for defending themselves.

The legal system is especially harsh and unsympathetic to Black female victims of intimate partner violence. When a clinical diagnosis of post-traumatic stress disorder is needed to prove innocence in a case of self defence, stereotypes work against Black women. There are few health care providers and therapists who specialize in the unique socio-economic and cultural challenges that Black survivors face, leaving women in the hands of professionals who use a one-size-fits-all model to address Black women's experiences with abuse. And if a Black woman's abuser is a Black man, she is further ostracized by her community for choosing her gender over her race—a traitor, a contributor to the mass incarceration of Black men. If she is trans, she faces the threat of even more violence for speaking up.

But it isn't just race that complicates the idea of the perfect victim, it's age and marital status too. Historically, Canada has conducted research and funded programs for domestic violence within heterosexual couples, which involves women who are married legally or by common law, a group that is typically older. While studies on violence in university-age women were prevalent in the early '90s, research conducted over the past two decades has seldom included young unmarried people, or the unique factors that affect us: technology, trends in dating, social media, socio-economic status. Surprisingly, it's not older women who are most at risk of partner violence in this country—it's young, often university-age women. Statistics Canada says that young women between the ages of twenty and twenty-four have the highest rate of experiencing intimate partner violence (IPV), and we are six times more likely to experience partner violence than our male counterparts of the same age.

The cases across North America feel endless. In May 2010, twenty-two-year-old University of Virginia student Yeardley Love was beaten to death by a former boyfriend. In the days before her death, he sent her threatening emails, including one after an altercation that said, "I should have killed you." In July 2010, twenty-three-year-old Ryerson University student Carina Petrache was stabbed multiple times by her boyfriend, who then set fire to the rooming house where they both lived in separate apartments. In September 2011, nineteen-year-old student Maple Batalia was gunned down by her ex-boyfriend in a parkade on Simon Fraser University's Surrey campus. In September 2012, eighteen-year-old Alexandra Kogut from SUNY Brockport was beaten to death by her boyfriend with a curling iron. In February 2014, twenty-one-year-old Olivia Greenlee was shot in her car by her fiancé, a fellow student at Union University. That September, Shao Tong, a twenty-year-old Iowa State University international student, was strangled to death by her boyfriend and stuffed into the trunk of her own car. In February 2015, twenty-one-year-old Miami University student Rebecca Eldemire was shot in her face by her ex-boyfriend as she slept. In March 2016, twenty-two-year-old University of Washington student Katy Straalsund was beaten to death by her boyfriend after they allegedly took LSD together. As he choked her, he repeatedly shouted, "I will kill you."

In August 2017, nineteen-year-old Kwantlen Polytechnic student Kiran Dhesi was found dead in a car that was set on fire; her boyfriend was charged with her murder two years later. In October, twenty-year-old University of Pittsburgh student Alina Sheykhet was killed by her ex-boyfriend in her off-campus home. Before her death, she had filed a restraining order against him after he broke into her house. In October 2018, twenty-one-year-old University of Utah track athlete Lauren McCluskey was kidnapped outside her dorm and found shot dead in a parked car on campus, killed by her ex-boyfriend. They had broken up after she found out he lied about his name, age, and status as a sex offender. After her death, the university was under investigation for not filing a formal complaint for nearly a week after McCluskey gave them proof he was extorting and stalking her. In 2019, twenty-year-old Skylar Williams was abducted from Ohio State University's Mansfield campus by Ty'Rell Pounds, her ex-boyfriend and the father of her child. He held her at gunpoint and forced her into a car. They both died after a police chase and shootout, but it was Pounds's gun that killed Williams. They had a toxic relationship that started in high school.

Many of these young women had already left their killers. Some had confided in loved ones and friends that they were scared. Several had reported previous incidents like harassment and stalking to the police. All of these deaths could have been prevented. These are only a few of the cases that made headlines, and they barely represent the huge number of young women who are killed by their partners.

The alarming rate of intimate partner violence in Millennial women's relationships is shocking, given our generation's action towards social causes. Young women are spearheading discussions on a variety of women's issues. We storm our campuses rallying for sexual assault prevention and we demand rapists be held accountable. We organize events such as SlutWalk and continue older ones like Take Back the Night. We engage in Twitter campaigns like #IBelieveYou, #MeToo, and #TimesUp to bring attention to violence against women. We write first-person stories about our experiences with sexual assault and misogyny on websites dedicated to centring women's voices. This generation still honours Carol Hanisch's statement, "the personal is political," while making every cause more intersectional than the last. We show up for one another. Yet we haven't rallied around partner violence in the same way, despite it being so prevalent among young women.

Partner violence in young people's relationships has never been taken seriously because many young adults are still dating; this doesn't carry the same social status as the legally binding commitment of marriage. However, in many ways, Millennials face more obstacles to safety than the previous generation. The stigma women experience for casually dating, being non-monogamous or sexually fluid makes it harder for us to come forward, or to know if we even fit into the rigid category of what defines "partner" violence. Unaffordable housing and an unstable job market mean young people are moving in together faster than ever, and might stay with an abuser because they can't afford to live on their own. Partners can cyberbully us with abusive messages and threats, and ruin our lives with intimate photos or defamatory comments that live on the internet forever. Social media lets people share their lives—and locations—with the tap of an icon, making us more prone to online and physical stalking. And the numbers don't lie: cyber violence, which includes threats, harassment, and stalking, is more prevalent among women aged eighteen to twenty-four. Our bruises are visible: dark, painful reminders that we wear on our bodies, markers of our collective trauma—and they are not healing. But does anyone notice?

/ / /

Stacks of research and yellow U.S. calling cards littered my desk in my Toronto apartment as I tried to piece together what contributed to my generation of women becoming the most victimized age group in Canada when it came to intimate partner violence. I had chosen the topic for my thesis in my final year of my Master of Journalism program at Ryerson. It had been two years since I moved away from London to start the next chapter of my life, and five years since I last saw Joshua. Now, in my early twenties, I was still working through the trauma of our relationship. I wondered how long the emotional wounds would last; I still felt its shadow over me, and yet now that I was finally ready to get counselling, I had aged out of most programs' period of eligibility for survivors of violence. I was searching the internet for where to find help, when I came across the Statistics Canada study about young women's rates of victimization. I wanted to find out why this was happening, and I wanted to speak to women, especially the ones like me—in a post-secondary school, who knew the red flags and cycle of violence, who had the support of their family but still ended up in an abusive relationship. I wanted to know if they still carried that trauma with them too.

I put call-outs on social media and asked friends and former professors to circulate it. Dozens of women in university contacted me, wanting to share their stories. I did hours of interviews. We cried and we laughed. We spoke openly and honestly. Sometimes we sat in silence. The interviews were emotional and draining, and yet all of us, strangers to each other, had been connected by these moments that had changed our lives.

There were so many: a student whose chivalrous boyfriend started to control her clothing, body, and friendships, then stalked her when she broke it off; a quiet girl who stayed with her emotionally abusive boyfriend because he hadn't hit her—until he did; a polyamorous young woman who couldn't afford to move out of her abusive primary partner's house; a woman raped by the man she had just started dating; a woman whose friend-with-benefits orchestrated her gang-rape; a woman who was repeatedly assaulted by the father of her child and held at knifepoint (she's still in hiding with her son, who she named after an angel).

Experts explained to me that the independence of moving away from home also creates a fear of confiding in or relying on parents for help; that friends are just as uneducated and uncertain about what constitutes violence. Concerned professors who teach courses on violence against women told me the students who participate the most in class are the same ones who come to their office hours to ask if what their boyfriend did was abuse. They wondered why there were so many services for sexual assault when intimate partner violence is just as common.

I also came across Gaye Warthe, the Chair of the Department of Child Studies and Social Work at Mount Royal University in Calgary. In 2010, she created Stepping Up, a peer-facilitated dating-violence prevention program for post-secondary students in Canada, which she called the first of its kind in the country. She listed a variety of reasons why university-age people are at risk of violence: being unsure about what constitutes abuse; societal beliefs about the superficiality of young people's relationships; the delegitimizing of university relationships by society and health care providers because of the belief that students are always having the best time of their lives; and, most importantly for young women, not seeing their needs represented in current domestic-violence resources such as shelters, which young women believe are for women who are married or have kids. We also talked about the funding gap: programs for teens are prevalent, but they end at eighteen. Other programs are funded to cater to married and cohabitating women, who are often older. Funding for violence intervention and prevention in the demographic I belonged to was sparse.

Few resources exist to help young, university-age women wanting to leave their partners in the aftermath of an assault. So, we turn to our friends, but they're just as uninformed as us. Some of us turn to our parents, but often they can offer nothing more than to suggest going to the police. Police may press charges if they take us seriously—if we are the "ideal" victims. Otherwise, reports will collect in a file until it's too late. We'll be told to call back if he does something to us again. We accept this and wait—watching over our shoulder when walking home; installing a second lock on the door; gripping a key between our fingers on the way to our car—hoping he doesn't show up again. Hoping he doesn't kill us this time.

/ / /

Somewhere between wishing for death and hoping for justice, I fought for life.

Three months had passed since I last saw Joshua, and I had barely left the house. From my bed, I scrolled through my Facebook feed, which was bloated with photos of people jumping into pools in backyards and at all-inclusive resorts in the Caribbean. Everyone had gone on without me. And as my nineteenth birthday passed—a miserable, uneventful day—I made one wish: I would not let another year of my life go by like this again.

I needed to move my body. It was heavy to carry around, a toxic sludge of anger and anxiety. I decided to try a hot yoga class. The studio had a dark wood finish and large mirrors, with heat panels across the ceiling that glowed orange-red. The sweltering heat was unbearable; I couldn't breathe, and I slid around on my cheap mat the whole session. But it was the most in touch I had felt with my body in a long time. I could feel every itch on my damp skin, every drop of sweat that trickled down my jawline, every breath enter and leave my lungs, like I was purging months of sadness. In that discomfort, I felt connected to myself.

I went to yoga nearly every day, pushing myself to more challenging limits. I got a job that I loved, and I started to come out of my shell again, seeing my friends and spending time with family, wearing my shorts, skirts, and dresses, my bare legs free and sun-kissed in the summer heat. I dropped Social Work to pursue majors in English and Women's Studies. I wanted to learn about the ways that the patriarchy harms women long before they are even hurt; how it trickles into our daily lives, how it changes us. And now I had clarity about what I wanted to do after I graduated: I wanted to write about women, the subtle and explicit ways that we are under constant attack socially, racially, economically, and politically, and how these all work together to maintain our oppression. I also added a Certificate in Writing so I could start working on my portfolio. I made a promise to myself: I would never again let anybody stop me from living my life the way I wanted.

My outlook had completely changed: life could be taken at any moment, and now I knew that. I mourned for the innocence and naïveté with which I had moved through the world. Whether I was ready or not, I had irrevocably changed.

In the last week of summer, I packed up my things and

moved into the new, charming baby-blue house that Taz and I were renting in London. We painted our rooms—mine a calming lavender and Taz's a rich, hot pink—and put up artwork and tapestries around the house.

It was our home, and there were no rules—no parents, no boys, no curfew. I was ready to have the best year yet, to take another shot at being a fun, careless nineteen-year-old.

Most of all, I was ready to start doing what students in London were best known for: partying.

The Token Friend

WHAT TO EXPECT: You are the only thing that stands in the way of your white friends' love of rap music. And they sure do love the word nigga. In fact, they are *just dying* to shout it out when their favourite Kendrick Lamar song comes on. When your white crew gets turnt at a club or kegger, they'll approach you like a child wanting permission to watch another hour of TV and ask if "it's okay to say the N-word," which puts you in a difficult situation. Say yes and live with the decision you made when your friends take every possible opportunity to use it. Say no and you become the bitch that killed their vibe.

They may also refer to you as their "Black friend," making you the vessel through which they become cultured; and by association, you become an honorary white person (and they won't let you forget they've gifted you with this honour). In taking part in this friendship, you've unknowingly signed up for a lifetime of inappropriate, offensive, and unfunny Black jokes, which your friends think they are entitled to make. When they meet another Black person at a house party, they will try to set you two up even though you don't even know each other. They will watch from afar to see if you get on. It's like being surrounded by farmers waiting for their two horses to sniff each other and mate.

HOW TO DEAL WITH IT: When people see you hanging around with your white friends, it may evoke feelings of pity or sadness. Ignore this, they think you're being held captive. They'll wonder if you're whitewashed, or worse— brainwashed à la *Get Out* (you might be, but that's for a different book). Don't let friendship stop you from unleashing hell when your white friends start their sentences with "I'm not racist but . . ." or letting them know that being friends isn't an invitation to touch your hair (why do they love to do that?) and talk with a Blaccent.

party
gastritis

The first rule Taz and I learned in second year is that partying in London is always justified. There isn't much else to do in the city, so you drink for just about anything: good grades, good (or bad) sex, an interesting conversation, bumping into an ex, finding a lottery ticket on the ground, Alexander Keith's birthday. You drink anything, too, as long as it's potent enough: coolers, whiskey, rye, rum, tequila, any kind of questionable mixed drink. But vodka was our drink of choice. We didn't stay in touch with many kids from our dorm floor who were having house parties and keggers, but that didn't bother us—we still had Malcolm, who came out with us sometimes, and there was a whole outside world when 11 p.m. hit. By the end of September, we had gotten into a groove: after class we'd come home, nap, shower, shave, and get ready to go out. As we pre-drank, and I played the songs from my curated party playlist, we'd do our hair and makeup and pick an outfit. Then we'd run out of the house—lipstick tube in mouth, one stiletto in hand—to catch the last bus of the night at 11:21 p.m. The driver always slowed down; he knew we were coming.

Sometimes we bar-hopped, heading down to Jim Bob's, where someone wearing plaid was guaranteed to throw up on me; Joe Kool's, a bustling bar full of mature clientele; the Ceeps, an infamous student hangout where the parents of current students met once upon a time; Cobra, a short-lived techno club full of good-looking Arabs and Italians; or our favourite, Jack's, where the cheap drinks and packed dance floor were a hit with students and locals alike. It was one of the only places that played hip-hop, and so it was one of the few places where we saw faces like ours—at least on some nights. Each weekend, it was full of people who we came to recognize as regulars, whose names we never got to know.

At Jack's, we had a place to go, to look forward to. The attention we received as some of the only women of colour on nights out felt advantageous. We were a duo, known as the two brown girls (or two Black girls, depending on who said it). If we got separated, strangers pointed us in the direction of each other. The bouncers let us cut the line. If a guy wanted to buy one of us a drink, he knew he'd have to buy two. When a hip-hop or dancehall song played, groups of men would swarm, standing around us in a circle, their arms outstretched, whistling, grabbing, waiting for a turn that wouldn't come. We were the "Mary Kate and Ashley" when the DJ played "Niggas in Paris." *The brown twins. The dark ones.*

We danced and sang all night, our hair matted to our foreheads, screaming like the white girls around us when our favourite song came on. We'd realize where we were, that we didn't have to go back home, that we no longer had to dream of this moment, this freedom, and Taz would grab my hands, her eyes wide and glistening. "We're here," she'd say, almost on the verge of tears. We wore our anticipation of the night in the goosebumps that ran across our skin; in the one-night friendships that always felt like they could thrive outside those walls; in the bravado of flirting with someone cute; in the agency to regularly take part in a scene that, back home, was usually reserved for special occasions. We were running free and wild in the night, completely unrestrained and uninhibited. I never wanted it to end.

We looked forward to the walks home, where we'd meet more people or eye-roll as groups of men followed, begging for just a minute of our time. If we were broke, we'd stand by the Little Caesars and flirt with anyone holding a box of pizza, a surefire way of getting a slice. If we could tolerate the long line of drunk people at Giorgio's, we'd get our own. We'd head to the food truck parked by the train tracks on Richmond Street, and catch up with the older Greek man who always gave us extra garlic dip. But most nights we'd eat at the Indian restaurant up the street, run by two young Sikhs who made the most delicious curries. It was always empty at that hour, so we would sit and chat with them while we ate.

This was our new routine. There was so much excitement, so much possibility, so much to look forward to every night. We could do whatever we wanted, wear what we pleased, be who we were. Taz and I had felt invisible for so long. But under the bright lights and with the sheen of sweat on our dancing bodies, we were two girls who were more seen than ever before.

/ / /

By the time the chilly November air arrived with the southwestern front, Taz and I were partying nearly every day. Some Fridays, we pulled all-nighters at a club, then headed to grab our bags so we could catch the first Greyhound bus back home. When we saw our hometown friends, we'd tell them tales of nights out: the parties, the people, the freedom. They'd say we were living the ultimate life. When strangers asked if Western really was a party school, we'd enthusiastically confirm.

This new world gave me a chance to try my hand at casual dating, and I was seeing a few guys I met at bars. But even that couldn't stop me from thinking about Joshua.

I functioned throughout the day, busy with school, but at night his presence lurked in the darkness, reminding me that I was spoiled goods, that no one would ever love me after being in a relationship like ours. Each time I went out and wore the clothes he would hate, drank more than he would want, flirted with a new guy, it felt like a defiant *fuck you*, like I was capable of moving on and he had no power to stop me. I drank more and more each night, trying to drink him into oblivion, trying to drink myself into the arms of someone else.

After the assault, the way I perceived men had changed. As a painfully shy and introverted teen, I had put men on a pedestal. But now I equated men with pain, which somehow made them seem more human, approachable. I both wanted to date men and stay far away from them, a complex and conflicting, post-traumatic response that frustrated me as much as it did the men I was involved with. One moment, I was giving out my number to a guy I was interested in; the next, I was cowering in the corner of my room when he called. I found it impossible to recognize a normal interaction when I was irrationally suspicious of everything. Drinking was a way to numb myself to my unpredictable emotions, though it was in vain; the terror always set in.

I didn't want to get hurt again, so I closed myself off to being open and vulnerable, stopping any chance at a healthy relationship before it could happen. And despite my lack of trust in men, I was desperate to prove that my relationship had not ruined me. Against my better judgement, I dove head first into anything that seemed to have a fraction of a possibility, ignoring the mixed messages, just so I could prove to myself that I could move on, just like Joshua had.

I gravitated to men who were selfish and emotionally unavailable. They were there at night when I needed them, without pressuring me for a commitment. To reward them for their non-intrusiveness, I maintained the illusion of being passive, letting them walk all over me, listening to their problems, being the "cool girl" they were searching for.

Each time the tequila settled and the familiar dread of sobriety hit, I hushed it with more alcohol. I couldn't stand being alone with myself, with this anger and fear that was so devastating. I wanted to be a normal functioning girl again, a carefree girl, a happy girl. I wanted to stop hurting people and myself.

I wanted it to be like it was before, but there was nothing to go back to.

///

After leaving London's Club 181 on King Street in the fall of 2002, a Black female student noticed a white man standing in front of the bar as she tried to hail a cab. She was intrigued by his shirt, decorated with skulls and writing in a language she didn't recognize.

Curious, she approached him. "What does your shirt say?" she asked. His friend, another white man, came over and got in her face.

"What the fuck are you talking to him for?" he yelled. Quickly, she backed away, telling them that she was leaving. They grabbed her; the man in the skull shirt punched her in the face.

They walked away from her, as she bled. The man in the shirt turned back around. "And the shirt says, 'I hate motherfucking niggers.'"

Ten years later, just a few blocks away, Taz and I were outside Jack's after a night out, looking for a cab. Two white men were standing at the side of the building smoking a cigarette when they started hitting on her, following us as we walked down the street. Taz tried to turn them down politely.

"We just want to talk to you, what's wrong with that?" one of the men, muscular with a blond crop, said as he grabbed her arm.

She was losing her self-confidence in the face of their aggression. I stepped in. "Can you leave her alone? She's not interested."

"No one's talking to you. We're talking to your friend," he said harshly in his Eastern European accent.

"Well, she doesn't want to talk to you. You can see she's uncomfortable." I put my hand on Taz's back to guide her away. He let go of her arm and turned towards me, inches from my face. His laughing friend half-heartedly held him back.

"Why don't you go back to your third-world country, bitch?" he yelled at me.

I yelled something back about the irony of a white man with an accent telling me to go back to some non-descript place when I was born here.

"I should beat you up for even daring to speak to me." He came closer as Taz guided me towards home. They followed us, still threatening me. I couldn't show them my fear. They walked behind us for a few blocks before turning around and heading south.

Ten years separated these incidents. Ten minutes was the distance between where they happened. And in their eerie similarities, it was as if nothing had changed at all.

Taz and I never spoke about what happened that night. During the confrontation, she was laughing at its absurdity. But that didn't ease my feelings about being an unwanted visitor. We were getting used to men's attempts to hit on us by bringing up race: that they had never danced with a Black or brown woman before; that their friend once dated a woman like us and they wanted to know what it was like. However, we experienced these sexually racist pickup lines in different ways. Around town, brown women and white men were one of the more common interracial pairings we'd seen. To men, Taz was still exotic, but they were used to seeing women like her. They saw her as passive, smart, respectable enough.

For me, the conversations veered directly into stereotypes: addressing me as Boo, Ma, Ebony, or Chocolate. The verbs were endless: "I've never danced with/fucked/spoken to/ touched/seen/talked to/dated/kissed a Black girl." If I rejected an advance, I was a Black bitch. If we talked about my multiracial background, they'd focus on me being Jamaican and "Black enough," adding a wink. They called me Beyoncé, Solange, Nicki Minaj. Sometimes men would stand in front of me, staring at me with a smirk as they hit on me, their friends laughing behind them. Sometimes they said nothing, only leered. Many of the men Taz met wanted to get to know her, but most men wanted to know what I was like in bed. White guys who approached her at the bar would gently pull her aside to talk, or take her on dates during the day. Meanwhile, men were either approaching me to make a racist remark and leave, or to ask if it was true that "Once you go Black, you never go back." As men put their hands on the small of Taz's back, they were shoving me out of the way.

Men treated me with a mix of hypersexuality and animalistic aggression, pushing me around like I was less than a woman, less than human. They were quick to anger around me, quick to threaten me with physical harm just for opening my mouth.

One of these men was a big dude—a tall and burly Rick Ross look-alike twice our age. His face, dark and glistening with sweat, didn't crack a smile as he towered over Taz, who just minutes ago, was standing alone as I went to get us drinks. "Yo, Indian girl, you're so sweet, let me talk to you," he said as he swiped at her like a bear blindly trying to catch a fish in a pond.

"Can you leave her alone? You're making her uncomfortable," I said. He swatted me out of the way.

"I'm trying to talk to your friend," he said in his deep voice.

I put myself in front of her. "She clearly doesn't want to talk to you."

He turned around to face me, several inches taller than me, so close I could smell the saltiness of his sweat. "Mind your business."

"It's my business if you're harassing my friend." I led Taz away from the crowd, but he grabbed her other arm, yanking her back. Taz was silent, her eyes wide and fearful in the middle of this tug of war. Eventually, we broke free. We were both shaken up and decided to go home.

As we crossed the street, a black suv screeched, sharply turning onto the road, speeding towards me at nearly sixty kilometres an hour. Its lights blinded me as the driver floored it.

Taz pulled me out of the way but the suv swerved towards me, roaring as it accelerated, headlights blinding me. It mimicked my pattern as I moved forward and stepped backward. When it got close enough that I could see past its beams, I saw him behind the wheel—the guy from the bar. I had poked the fucking bear.

I wasn't going to let him intimidate me. I stood in the road, drunk with liquid bravado as he sped closer, the people around me gasping and squealing.

I closed my eyes, waiting for the end. The car was revving. It was charging towards me. Then it stopped, barely a millimetre from my shin.

He rolled down his window, contorted his fat fingers into a gun shape and pointed it at me, all while looking me dead in the eyes. "Nigga Mercy!" he yelled before rolling the window back up, swerving around me, and driving off.

This man, who I'm guessing was trying to tell me that he had done me the honour of saving my life instead of running me over because we were both Black, was set on making me pay for not allowing him to sexually harass my friend. After that night, we'd still see him around Jack's, but he never spoke to Taz again. Instead, he'd bump into me on purpose, spilling my drink. Ignoring him seemed to annoy him more. He lurked in the corner, in my direct line of sight, glaring at me with hatred. I was the woman who had refused to give in to his entitlement, and it enraged him.

One thing was clear about nights out with Taz: I was the punching bag for men. Perhaps it was our physical makeup: Taz, with her small, straight nose, long straight jet-black hair, tiny thin lips, and flushed pink cheeks, combined with her rich dark skin and long legs, was a brown Barbie doll. I had a wide nose and full lips, thick thighs, and head full of big curls. For every great night at Jack's, I spent another against the wall with a drink in my hand feeling uncomfortable—about my appearance, my place here.

I was starting to understand that these weren't coincidences; this was my reality. This was how misogynoir—the cocktail of racism and sexism that Black women experience—functioned. And this was how people valued my life and my humanity, if at all.

I was angry with myself for not being able to forget about these interactions and just enjoy the night, like Taz. And I felt scared, especially a few hours in, when inebriation made people vulgar, when the threat of violence or humiliation was too much to gamble on, and I'd resign myself to the few chairs at the back of the bar, wishing I was home in the comfort of my bed, while Taz danced.

Taz didn't understand my new reluctance about going out, and it was hard for me to explain that I felt both rejected and objectified—a target of the most sexualized comments *and* the most abusive. How could I be comfortable in a space where my presence not only made men want to sexualize me but hurt me too?

My nights out were reproducing the tokenism I felt in my classes, but here, whatever curiosity or disdain people had for me was magnified by alcohol. I drank more than before, unable to get drunk enough to stop feeling out of place. I drank until I was doubled over from the pain in my stomach.

But as I struggled to come to terms with how I felt on our nights out, Taz was settling into her new life as a party girl. She thought she'd never have this kind of freedom. Her mother called every day, begging her to come home, saying that she had made a mistake letting her leave. She wanted Taz to transfer to a nearby school and start the process of an arranged marriage.

Taz was making up for lost time, and trying to do everything before it was up, living faster than I could keep up with. Part of me was jealous of how she was able to move through this space—beautiful, carefree, no damns given about the consequences. She didn't worry about her safety, about feeling uncomfortable or rejected. But I had misunderstood her recklessness as fearlessness. We were both out of control, in different ways. We were just too scared to admit it to each other.

/ / /

As I realized the new life I was bragging about wasn't all it was made out to be, I was also trying to figure out a new but persistent pain in my stomach. It started as a twinge around Halloween, accompanied by bloating so pronounced that I looked six months pregnant. I sucked in my stomach when I zipped up my dresses and skirts, hoping the pain would go away on its own.

It was in the top part of my belly, sometimes stabbing, sometimes a dull ache. As we continued to party throughout the winter, I found myself drenched in sweat and gripping my stomach after only a few sips. The pain started to last all day.

That February, seventeen-year-old Trayvon Martin was walking through a gated community in Florida when he was shot and killed by George Zimmerman. Zimmerman claimed defence; Martin was only carrying an Arizona fruit cocktail and a bag of Skittles from the convenience store he had just left.

The news of Martin's death added to my fears about violence escalating, especially when Taz and I were out at night. I worried about what it meant to look "suspicious," always aware of how my body could be interpreted as up to no good. It was a label often used against Black men—a signifier of being out of place, not from here, bad news. But from the way employees eyed me in a store when I picked something up, the women who looked nervously over their shoulders when I walked behind them, to the glimmer of fear in the eyes of people when my voice loudened in excitement, every action felt like it had the potential to get me in trouble even as a woman. The thoughts came in a flurry everywhere I went: *Do not look suspicious. Do not act suspicious. Do not raise your voice. They will call the police. They will hurt you. That boy only had Skittles.* The agonizing pain in my stomach seemed to worsen with every worrisome thought, as if my brain and belly were fused together.

Weeks after the news of Trayvon Martin's death, I went to the campus doctor's office. The pain had become so unbearable that I couldn't even get up for class. A blond nurse in her late thirties examined me on the table. "Does this hurt?" she asked each time she pressed on my stomach, and each time I said "yes," the pain lingered, even after she moved to the next location.

"Do you drink? Maybe when you're out with your friends?" she asked.

"Yes, but only socially," I said, wincing at her fingers digging into my upper belly.

"How many drinks would you say? Do you drink pop as a mixer too?"

I paused. I had never counted how many drinks I was having. I replayed a typical night in my head: *two, five, seven, eight*. I thought about more recent nights: *eleven, twelve*. "Eight to thirteen a night. With pop as the chaser," I sputtered. She quickly removed her gloves and looked at me, almost impatiently.

"Honey, you have gastritis," she said. "It's the inflammation of the lining of your stomach, and binge-drinking makes it worse."

"I'm not a binge drinker," I pushed back.

"You're drinking well above the recommended number of drinks for a woman your age. I see this all the time, it's quite common among students."

Stress was the main factor in my gastritis, she told me, not the actual drinking itself. "What are you so stressed about? Identifying it would help you work on how to manage it."

I thought about how I would explain it to her: how does someone deal with the kind of stress that comes with feeling unwelcome and unwanted? When your grades are slipping because it's easier to spend hours getting drunk to forget about how misunderstood and hated you feel in this city and on this campus? How about when your ex is haunting you and you've made yourself a doormat for the men you're seeing, and everywhere you go you're reduced to a body part or a racist joke? Or when the only good friend you have, your anchor to home, doesn't understand any of this and is slipping away, and the only time you talk anymore is when the night comes? What about when you can't tell if you need cognitive behavioural therapy to stop thinking that you're going to get assaulted, or if that's actually your new reality? What kind of remedy is there when you're in such a dark place that you're afraid for yourself—of yourself? How, Doctor, should I aim to manage that kind of stress?

"I've just had a hard time adjusting to my second year," I said, and she didn't ask questions. She prescribed me some medication, told me to lay off the booze, stress, and acidic foods, and sent me on my way.

To deal with my own binge drinking, I first had to make peace with the term. I *was* a binge drinker. I drank past my limits, past the discomfort in my stomach, to have a good night or to forget a bad one. I drank to feel numb and to cope with the rejection I felt at school and during our nights out.

Gastritis is a chronic issue, sentencing me to a lifetime of pain if I didn't get it under control. During the first few weeks after my diagnosis, I still went out with Taz at night, sipping water, but I often succumbed to a drink or two, which I deeply regretted when my stomach reacted angrily. After class I researched how to manage gastritis and what foods to avoid. I cooked my own meals instead of filling up on the spicy curries and greasy pizza we usually ate after the bar. To manage stress, I went back to yoga, which helped with the worrying thoughts that were out of my control. And when I craved the spoils of my old lifestyle, the thought of living with this immobilizing pain for the rest of my life was enough to keep me on track.

Without a drink in my system, I got to see the inner workings of the bar scene, the ways white men took up space, jumping up and down on the dance floor, pushing and stepping on people, spilling their drinks on girls. The way they goaded each other and drank until they were puking on unsuspecting patrons. How they pulled out a joint in the middle of the dance floor with ease, only sometimes ripped from the crowd by a bouncer. How groups of white men schemed before sending one of their friends over to talk to the token woman of colour as the others laughed. *Do you date white men? Where are you really from? I've never talked to a Black girl.* I was repulsed by the swaying, glassy-eyed men who approached me, some of whom just stood in front of me, staring, smirking, leering.

Nightlife is one of the main places young white men try out their privilege and entitlement. In this show of heterosexual dominance, they perform for their other straight friends, harassing and targeting the groups they see as inferior—women, LGBTQ2S+ people, and bodies of colour—to maintain the respect and friendship of other men.

Sober, I watched men slip their hands up women's dresses or grab the drunkest woman that walked by. I saw men feeding drinks to women already well past their limit. In the alleys and on the sidewalks, women lay incapacitated from alcohol and roofies, sometimes alone and crying, other times unable to cry out as the arm of a sober-looking man held them too close, promising that he'd get them home safely.

When Taz and I saw a girl who was under the influence, wandering around on her own or unable to even stand, we'd get her a cab, or at least back to her friends. It would take some time for me to understand that some of those women hadn't just had too much to drink but had their drinks spiked. I don't how many women's lives I witnessed being forever changed in seedy bars.

Nightlife is dangerous for women, but it's also dangerous for anyone who isn't a straight white man. Over the years I've received messages from all kinds of nightlife-goers in London: from queer people who had been beaten and harassed by bouncers and patrons, and Black people who weren't let into bars because of their attire. Former bouncers told me their managers asked them not to let Black people in because they don't buy drinks. DJs at popular bars shared stories about their bosses demanding they not play hip-hop because it attracts "trouble." Meanwhile, white guys started fights that spilled into the streets, kicking and head-butting each other, covered in dirt and blood. They openly groped women. Nobody thought they were violent or rowdy. Nobody thought they were trouble.

People of colour know they don't have the luxury of blaming alcohol for acting foolish at a bar. We know that our bodies and our behaviour are always being policed. We don't get an automatic welcome to the party—we are constantly having to prove that we deserve an invitation. Even then, we know it can be revoked at the first slip-up. For many of us, the misinformed message of respectability—trying to show that we aren't a stereotype and that our values and currency are on par with white people's—is reiterated by our parents, churches, and communities. If we achieve this, we are told, we will be welcomed by white people. If we act more like them, we will get half as far. Being respectable means that as a child and a young adult, acting foolish isn't an option. We must act right, talk right, keep ourselves grounded, even as our white counterparts dance on a bar, or jump up in the air and push each other during their favourite EDM song like they're in a mosh pit. We know that one wrong move will undo all our hard work. One wrong move could be labelled "suspicious." It could get us taken down by bouncers. It could get us arrested or tasered. It could get us killed.

When white people behave badly, it's an individual trait. When people of colour misbehave, it's a problem with the entire race. White people get the green light to be hedonistic, carefree, flawed. Our culture loves to romanticize young, beautiful, and brooding drug-and-alcohol-addicted white people. There's been a boom in addiction memoirs by white women—Cat Marnell's *How to Murder Your Life*, Jowita Bydlowska's *Drunk Mom*, Lisa F. Smith's *Girl Walks Out of a Bar*, Melissa Broder's *So Sad Today*, and Sarah Hepola's *Blackout: Remembering the Things I Drank to Forget*. Can you imagine a woman of colour writing a memoir about being passed out drunk in the bushes and then still having a job to go to in the morning? How about a Black mother who leaves her child unattended to drink without having them taken away by Children's Aid?

We know we're not afforded that privilege.

Films about university and Greek life are not missing from our cultural repertoire: *American Pie, Accepted, Neighbours, Van Wilder, The House Bunny*. Coming to Western, I wanted the type of experience I'd seen over and over again in films and TV shows and on Instagram feeds. But I now knew that it wasn't a coincidence that those experiences were always about white students. When white people get wasted in public or do drugs, they're having fun or finding themselves. Or, they're poor souls from a good family who deserve sympathy and redemption. When Black people do it, they're criminals who deserve to do hard time.

White students can do worrying things at night because they know they'll be protected. Whether it's conscious or not, that is white privilege.

It is a privilege not to worry about looking stupid or getting too drunk. It is a privilege to misbehave or engage in criminal acts in public, and have people see it as so non-threatening that there's no need to call the cops. It is a privilege to get a "slap on the wrist." Meanwhile, young Black people are being stopped by police across North America for walking, sleeping, swimming, selling lemonade, going to class, picking up garbage. Killed for putting their hands in their pockets or for simply being in their own home. For being "suspicious-looking." White people can be suspects, but they are hardly ever viewed as suspicious.

In February 2015, Aaron Ferkranus, a twenty-six-year-old Black man, went into medical distress after being restrained by bouncers at the Thorny Devil nightclub in London for throwing a punch that temporarily knocked a white man unconscious. As the man was taken away by ambulance, bouncers kneed Ferkranus several times in the leg and pinned him down, keeping him there even after he stopped moving. While he was unresponsive and barely breathing, a police officer arrested him. When they did call the paramedics, Ferkranus had no vital signs. He was pronounced dead the next day. The Special Investigations Unit completed its investigation seven months later, clearing the officer in relation to Ferkranus's death and concluding that the cause of death is still unknown. The officer who was facing charges refused to participate in an SIU interview and refused to provide a copy of her duty notes, which is legal.

Black men are plagued by others' belief that they're brutish and dangerous, but a fight between white men is viewed as nothing more than a boys' scrap, even when blood streams from broken noses. It's that privilege that allows white men to dominate nightlife spaces, to assault without punishment, to make others feel unwelcome. And they laugh and joke while doing it.

And our culture tells them: where is the danger in that?

///

Spring arrived, and the departing winter took away the dirty, ciga-rette-filled snow banks and most of the city's student population.

London in May was quiet. Only locals and summer stu-dents strolled around during the day, and at night, clubs were near empty. I was taking two summer classes, the perfect excuse to not go out as much, opting for daytime nachos and evenings indoors watching movies. Taz quietly adapted to our new sched-ule, but to compromise we still went out on one weeknight, and on Saturdays.

As she tried on dress after dress, I did my course readings, only getting up to take a quick shower and put on a little makeup before we left. I relinquished my status as pre-drink DJ, so Taz got ready in silence. My fitted dresses and high heels remained in the closet as I threw on a T-shirt and jean shorts. Even the bus driver had stopped slowing down at our usual stop.

Like our new schedule, things weren't the same with Taz anymore. We used to scream in excitement when our favourite song came on; we'd dance with our arms slung around each other's shoulders, and we didn't care who else was around. Now Taz would dance with the guys who approached her, and I would hang out by the bar on my own, watching my surround-ings, watching her like a chaperone.

Choosing when I went out was one way I could control the amount of discrimination I experienced. I was finally able to see what I wasn't willing to before: Jack's was never my home. Nightlife was a seductive facade that made me believe I could fit in somewhere among the swirl of lights and sweaty bodies; that I could be that carefree, untouchable party girl. These possibilities seemed limitless in a dark room.

When you go home before the lights come on after a great night, you get to nurse the illusion, take it to bed with you, let it cuddle with your insecurities, your loneliness. But when the music stops and the lights abruptly turn back on, it's just a littered, beer-soaked dance floor.

Taz still had her haven, dancing in the dark with strangers, but it was no longer my refuge. The dim lights couldn't hide what I had seen.

The Token on Campus

WHAT TO EXPECT: You'll count how many Black
people you see on campus. And if you are lucky enough
to find others, you and your group of friends will be
stared at with fear and loathing for daring to even laugh
simultaneously. On your way to class, you'll pass by
wannabe hood handshakes and "What's up, nigga?"
greetings, signs of a strong bromance. White students
will not make room for you on the sidewalk—their
conversation is too important to be interrupted by
you—so you'll either be shoved as they barrel through
or you'll step off the sidewalk instinctively, and then
they'll look at you like *you're* the problem. Anywhere
you are on campus—walking through the field, at the
bookstore, in line for coffee, at the library—you will get
pushed, shoved, ignored, hit in the head with a football:
all the things that happen when you're a ghost, apparently.
You're basically as invisible as you are hypervisible.

HOW TO DEAL WITH IT: Stink-eye is passive-aggressive
and still scary enough to get the job done without
confrontation. These people are perpetually shook—
adjusting to student life, constantly hungover, failing
Calculus, afraid of everything. Let them know they have
one more thing to fear by crossing you. When white
kids refuse to make room for you on the sidewalk, *do
not step off*. Jim Crow South etiquette is over. When people
bump into you, spook them by firmly letting them know
you aren't Casper. You're nobody's friendly ghost.

anthony, my italian greek tragedy

In my mandatory first-year Introduction to Narrative course, we read the classics like *Frankenstein*, *The Adventures of Huckleberry Finn*, and *Heart of Darkness* (a book I had to discuss as the only Black person in the room). We learned about the Romantic era and the Sublime, we read Kafka and Poe, and we braved the epics like *Gilgamesh*. A lot of this didn't impress me.

In second year, however, I took literature courses that did interest me: Twisted Sexuality, Post-Colonial Literature, Feminist Literary Theory, Indigenous Fiction. I saw myself represented in many of these stories, these texts that weren't in the canon, electives that were not required to complete your degree.

But I did love me some classical Greek tragedy. I had read *Oedipus Rex* in my Grade 12 Advanced English class, and was mesmerized by the sin and salaciousness contained within the slim volume. I loved the structure in which it unfolded, the satire of the era. In my courses, I devoured texts like *Electra*, *Antigone*, and *Agamemnon*, fascinated by the plot lines: revenge, sex, desire, lust, polygamy, scheming. I loved that every character's action, which was always a bad decision, had a reaction—a consequence to look forward to.

That's how I came to think of my relationship with Anthony. He was a Black guy in a white man's body, or so he liked to say. Our relationship, if you could even call it that, was so unfortunate that you might compare it to a Greek tragedy: I was the tragic hero who, with my hubris (my arrogance and foolishness), made a fatal error (misjudging a white guy's interest in me), thus resulting in suffering, self-enlightenment, your pity, and a cautionary tale to share with friends. The chorus is my common sense just shouting insults at me while I ignore it at my peril.

In typical Greek-tragedy style, it was fate that we met—without him, I probably wouldn't have started my career as a journalist so soon. So, here's to you, Anthony, and our contemporary drama. You cheeky, fateful bastard.

Prologue

We are here to witness a tragedy of the most tragic: the twenty-first century dating life of a modern woman of colour. It involves the disastrous combination of a twenty-three-year-old fuckboy and a nineteen-year-old female clown. What ensues is his fetishization of Black women, a pregnancy scare, bell hooks, and a lot of crying.

Act One

CHORUS: *Girl, I know you don't know what the hell is going on yet, but he don't look right. Just run, girl, RUN!*

Most evenings in October were warm enough to skip pantyhose. Taz and I had just left Jack's and were walking on Richmond Row, which had shut down traffic for Homecoming Weekend.

The streets were jammed with hundreds of drunk people trying to get home, and barely any taxis. By 2 a.m., the breeze was biting; we rubbed our palms along our thighs to keep warm as we walked north to find a cab.

In my first fatal error, I wore a cheetah-print dress that night.

CHORUS: *Gasp! A sign!*

A few months earlier I had read an essay by Black feminist scholar bell hooks in which she talks about the problem with Black female entertainers who wear animal print or writhe around in cages in music videos. It reinforces stereotypes, she says, about our primitive, animalistic sexual nature—our Otherness—which is packaged for white audiences. I knew better than to give in to the tropes. I was a bad feminist.

"Hi." The voice came from behind me.

I turned around and saw a white guy with dark hair and dark eyes. He wasn't wearing a jacket, just a T-shirt and jeans, looking mildly uncomfortable as the breeze beat through his clothing.

"Hi," I mumbled. Taz was now on the street, begging for a cab to stop.

"Your dress really caught my attention," he said.

CHORUS: *You see?*

"That's nice," I said as I waved frantically for a cab.

"I'm Anthony," he yelled over the whistling wind, and put his hand out. I reluctantly shook it, then turned back around and continued flailing my arms, desperately wanting to go home to my warm bed. I was not interested in freezing to death with this strange, smiling man who couldn't take a hint.

"Look, I know you're probably not interested, but can I have your number? I'd really like to take you out for breakfast tomorrow."

I had never been asked out for breakfast. Drinks, yes. Dinner, sometimes. But breakfast was a serious display of interest. The very act of waking up early after a night of drinking to treat a girl to a meal seemed thoughtful.

Then he reached out his arm and, with ease, hailed a cab.

"You take it. I'll wait for the next one," he said.

I looked to Taz for some backup, but she wasted no time in running towards the cab as it pulled up to the curb.

"So, can I have your number?"

I quickly recited it while I stuck my foot into the cab, shooing away the drunkards clawing at the door, and he texted me his.

"If you're bored, text me tonight," he said, as I got in and reached for the handle to pull the door shut. He stopped me. "I'll be waiting."

He shut the door and I watched him as we drove away.

We ended up texting until 6 a.m. In our flurry of messages, I mentioned that we were struggling to install our new showerhead. He was a handyman, and said he'd come install it later in the week. I wasn't sure about his intentions, but we definitely needed the help. We planned to meet Friday evening.

///

Anthony looked different in the daylight. He was tall, about six-foot-two, with a slender but soft build. His slightly receding hairline was negated by his boyish face—tiny dark eyes, puffy, rosy cheeks, full lips, and some light stubble. He wore dark Guess jeans and a crisp white T-shirt with a sprout of dark chest hair visible from the V-neck collar. In his left hand was a toolkit. He smelled like Adidas cologne and spearmint gum, which he chewed on with straight, white teeth.

"Hey." He didn't smile. I brought him into the bathroom and showed him the new showerhead.

We tried to engage in some small talk as he worked, but he was bright red and tight-lipped. I watched him install the new head, staring at his shoulder blades moving in his shirt. Just as we started talking about the weather, he twisted the cheap plastic of the showerhead too hard with the wrench and water shot out from all sides, spraying us both. He apologized furiously, all wet and laughing in his white shirt like a college girl on spring break. I got him a towel, trying not to look as he dried off. He insisted he get us a new showerhead, on him, and said he'd be back in an hour.

As soon as he left, Taz came running downstairs. "What's he like?" The truth was, I was uncomfortable. White guys had only ever approached me to say something racially charged. I was suspicious about his intentions, though he hadn't given me any reason yet to be alarmed.

When he returned, he brought an expensive showerhead for our bathroom, and a Starbucks coffee for me.

He finished his handiwork and we went to my room. I sat on my bed and he sat on my office chair. Breaking the showerhead also broke the ice—in a rapid exchange, we learned we had the same taste in books and music. We were also both Geminis. We spoke for hours, which we attributed to our zodiac sign. We joked about how Geminis love making up nicknames for people, so he decided to call me "E."

Anthony was second-generation Italian; he had never eaten tomato sauce out of a jar. Originally from Winnipeg, he had recently come to London to work at his uncle's plumbing company. He was older, out of school, and he had a job, a car, and his own apartment. He carried himself with confidence; I was intimidated.

As evening turned into night, there wasn't a single moment of silence. But I was still waiting for the deal-breaker: the mention that I was cute for a Black girl or that he loved Black people, like all the other white guys I'd met.

It didn't come.

Suddenly, Anthony jumped out of the chair. "I have to go," he said, grabbing his keys.

"Oh, uh—okay. I'll see you out." I tried to conceal my confusion as I went to get his coat and walk him to the door.

It was tense again as we went down the stairs. He put his shoes on quickly, without a word, and then looked at me.

"Bye," he said abruptly, and left.

I stood in the hall for a few minutes, not sure what had just happened, but by the time I went back up the stairs, I had received a text from him.

I'm being so standoffish because I'm currently in a long-distance relationship that's in the process of ending, and I want it to be completely over before I do anything.

Part of me was relieved this couldn't go any further, but that didn't stop me from feeling a sliver of disappointment.

I texted back. *No worries. Thanks for letting me know. You deal with your issues first and we'll talk when you're ready.*

He thanked me for understanding, and I jumped onto my bed, tossing my phone to the side. I wondered about all the things he hadn't said. Maybe she'd cheated? Broken his heart? Maybe they'd grown apart? Whatever it was, I was now curious about him.

Act Two

CHORUS: *Girl, you know something's up AND YOU STILL HERE? You a damn fool.*

What are you doing tonight?

It was the beginning of November, just a few weeks after Anthony told me about his relationship. He hadn't mentioned anything more about the situation with his girlfriend and I didn't press. He had been texting me platonically since he came over, always polite and formal—*Hey, how's your day going? What readings are you doing now? Hope you're doing well.* And when he started dropping hints—*I was wondering if you'd like to go for shisha or catch a movie?*—I remained firm in my decision not to see him until he told me that his relationship was over. I was casually seeing other people, though my mind kept bringing me back to our conversation in my bedroom.

I was getting ready to meet Taz and her friends at the bar to celebrate another long week, and I had already started with a few drinks of my own. Anthony was at his boss's wedding, so it must have been the alcohol that gave him the brazenness he needed to send this abrupt and suggestive message. There were none of the usual inquiries about my day.

I didn't respond.

Ten minutes later, he called me.

"E!" he slurred obnoxiously. There was loud music in the background. "What are you doing tonight? Can I see you?"

"I'm going to meet Taz at the bar and I know you don't like Jack's, so maybe another time?"

"No, that's fine. Wait for me, I'll get a cab." He hung up.

Did he want to hook up? It seemed that way, but I didn't know if I could go through with it. Nothing about it felt right. I wrestled with myself, pacing around the room, spritzing on another layer of perfume and then trying to remove it with unscented lotion, touching up my lipstick then wiping it off with the back of my hand. I dialed his number to cancel, but put the phone down.

My doorbell rang fifteen minutes later. Anthony was standing there, still in his suit. He was swaying, his eyes unfocused, with a hint of childlike fear. He looked me up and down. He leaned in to kiss me, and I moved away. "No. You have a girlfriend," I said, but he just stared at me, bored, like he knew this was the part of the night where I gave him the mandatory scolding.

I wanted to muster up the courage to tell him he needed to break up with his girlfriend first, like all the strong-willed and in-control women I idolized in movies. To command respect. But I had no willpower. I couldn't deny that I wanted whatever was about to happen.

Act Three

CHORUS: *Damn, chile, you really screwed this one up—but that's okay, we know you're impulsive and haven't yet been blessed with the truth that is Lizzo (or the reality that is* Get Out*).*

"Goddammit," Anthony sighed. Every time he said that, he sounded annoyed. *Gahhhd dammit.*

His gum, which he'd spat out the last time he was over, had blackened and stuck to my hardwood floor instead of to the bag in the garbage he was aiming for. Nickels and dimes were scattered everywhere. My room was lit only by amber Christmas lights; outside, the snow was still. His phone vibrated furiously with missed calls from his girlfriend.

"Can I smoke here?"

"No."

He lit a cigarette anyway, knowing I hated it. He frowned as he inhaled.

"Well, that was fun," he said, rolling onto his side.

I nursed the sinking feeling in my stomach that I had come to know well.

"Yep. Lots of fun."

After our first night together, Anthony still smelled like Adidas cologne and spearmint, but he was different. He went from calling every day to calling me every weekend, until it was just on Saturday nights to ask what I was doing later. Every time I deleted his number, he'd call me and I answered. There was no redeeming myself.

I wanted to cut him off completely, and in those moments, I hated him as much as I hated myself for the excuses I made. Sober, he'd ask me to tell him all about my life, sitting patiently by my feet, telling me that he wished he could be like me—creative, kind, fearless. But then he'd ask me if buying a $300 ring was a nice Christmas gift for his girlfriend, and I'd lose the bit of confidence I had just pathetically built up. He would sit beside me, stroke my hair, keep my fingers warm with his lips, tell me how he liked me so much. A minute later, he'd be laughing in my face, pushing me away, staring at me without even blinking.

"What?" I'd challenge him back with my eyes, but he wouldn't look away.

"Nothing," he'd say after a long pause. But then he'd frown.

"Goddammit." He'd frown and sigh again, piercing the heavy, provoking silence. He'd shake his head frantically, flailing around the room, throwing things on the ground as though trying to shut off his brain, laughing that wicked laugh. All the while, his eyes darted about, eyebrows always arched as if up to no good.

He was kind and then he was cruel, vulnerable and then abrupt, and I couldn't reconcile the two. How he could gently kiss me goodbye every time he left and then ignore me for days. Through all of it, he still held me like I would break, unaware that he had already crushed me into pieces.

///

Act Four

CHORUS: *The circus called. It's accepting applications for CLOWNS.*

On a frigid Saturday night at the end of November, Anthony called to invite me and Taz to Cobra. I declined; it was too cold to even fathom going out.

"Come on, E, don't be an old lady," he whined, already tipsy. "We have bottle service and VIP line bypass until 11:30. Be a Gemini, E. Be a fucking Gemini."

The last thing any Gemini wants to hear is that they're a party pooper. I looked at the time: 10:40. I was putting my zodiac sign to shame.

I told Taz to get dressed and I hopped in the shower, shaved my legs as fast as I could, and applied thick layers of grey and gold eyeshadow. We ran out—shoes half on, my jacket stuck in my skirt, Taz not even wearing a coat—and caught the bus by mere seconds, as usual.

We got to Cobra and went straight to the bouncer, passing the large line of complaining people. "It's for Eternity, plus one," I said.

The bouncer looked at the list, looked at me, looked at my plus-one, then back at the list. Finally, he let us through.

"E!" Anthony waved a hand at me. "That's our booth over there." He pointed towards the back-left corner of the club. "I'll meet you guys in a second."

There were a dozen Italians sitting in the booth. Behind them a glass case of decorative ceramic skulls with red lights flashed like a warning.

"Should we go over there?" Taz asked reluctantly.

"Well, yeah!" I said, confidently, so that Taz wouldn't sense my fear. "I mean, we did come all this way."

We walked up to the booth and said hello to everyone; only two people acknowledged us. The others stared at us and then at each other, perplexed. Then a miniature man with dark hair appeared out of nowhere and gave us two glasses.

"I'm Fabio, Anthony's friend," he said with a goofy smile. "Like the romance novels." He winked at Taz and told us to have a drink.

I was in the process of pouring us a heavy-handed measure of vodka when I noticed some women and their boyfriends staring and whispering.

A girl with blunt bangs and dark lip liner got up and approached us

"Um, sorry, but that's our alcohol and this is our booth." Her face twitched as she tried to hold in her smirk. Her girl-friends giggled like hyenas behind her.

I grinned as I kept pouring. "*Oh*, I know that. We're with Anthony—he invited us."

Her heavily lined lips dropped into a scowl, and she retreated back to her seat. I poured some orange juice into my cup, took a long, refreshing gulp, then topped us up so we could get drunk and dance on her boyfriend's bottle service–contribution money.

Around 1:00 a.m., when all I was seeing were flashing lights and those ceramic skulls that illuminated the faces of the glaring mean girls, Anthony grabbed me to him and whispered in my ear, "Come over to my place. Right now."

Panic killed my buzz. We always went to my house; he lived farther away from downtown, in a middle-class area of west London that I wasn't familiar with. "Can we go to my house instead?"

"No," he growled. "My place or forget it."

"How will I get home?"

"I'll drive you home in the morning when Fabio returns my car."

He was really good at that—being a Gemini. It was his way or nothing at all. I was getting curious about what his place looked like, anyway. I reluctantly agreed, and found Taz to let her know we were leaving.

On the street outside, the harsh wind lashed our bare legs as we tried to hail a cab for Taz. In her little black minidress, she crouched over and hugged herself, trying to get warm, cursing herself for not bringing her jacket.

"Here, take mine, I'll have a ride in the morning." I removed it and handed it to her, unable to feel the bitter winter wind with all the vodka burning through me, despite only wearing a hot pink miniskirt, a V-cut black tank top, and knee-high tan heeled boots.

Once the cab had arrived for Taz, we waved goodbye and got in our own. As we headed down to Anthony's condo, I watched the meter increase—$13, $22, $30. I looked outside at the unfamiliar buildings, the area sparse except for a few abandoned strip plazas and beige high-rises. With each quarter on the meter, I regretted my choice a little more.

"So you're sure you'll drive me home in the morning?" I confirmed.

"I'm sure—I'll call Fabio right now and remind him." Anthony pulled out his phone and dialed Fabio's number. I heard the phone ring several times. "He probably can't hear it right now. But the car will be at my place by 8 a.m."

My gut was telling me to take my ass back home, but I convinced myself that it was harder to explain tucking and rolling out of this cab fifteen minutes into the ride than to just go with it.

We went home and ravished each other.

The next morning, the sun peeked through the dark-brown wooden blinds, brightening up a bedroom I had only seen at night. It was the ultimate bachelor's pad, with dark brown furniture and beige carpet; everything tucked away nicely in the closet behind frosted glass sliding doors. I shuffled towards the bathroom and saw a scary, frizzy-haired monster staring back at me in the mirror. Black flakes of what had once been mascara were littered across my cheeks. My hair had turned into a mini-fro, and my lipstick was all over my chin like a bad rash. I tried to fix the frizz with water, but it only made it worse. I tried to wash my face with wet toilet paper so I didn't get makeup on his white towels, but that just added soggy white specks to my disaster of a dehydrated face.

Anthony was in the kitchen making breakfast, with all the necessary items out on the large, white-marble island.

"Bacon?" he asked, lifting the tongs towards me, a juicy piece dangling in the air.

"No thanks." I quickly wiped the drool from the corner of my mouth and looked away. "Um, is your car back?"

"Uh . . . no. Fabio hasn't returned any of my phone calls. He must be hungover."

I thought about the cab meter. The tuck and roll sounded real good right now.

"Don't worry, he should be here soon." Anthony waved his hand dismissively while shoving the bacon in his mouth. "I'll keep trying him."

He offered me one of his T-shirts to wear. An hour and a half and seven phone calls later, I was feeling like a kid whose parents had forgotten to pick her up from school as I heard Anthony leave voicemail after voicemail until Fabio's inbox was full.

"I don't think the car is coming back anytime soon." He

scratched the back of his neck. "Maybe you should call a cab now."

I blinked as far as the crust in my eyes would allow.

"Oh—right," I stuttered. "For sure. Okay."

I quickly gathered my belongings from his bedroom. He followed me in. I stuffed my phone into my pocket-sized clutch, picked my skirt off the carpet, and cleared my throat, waiting for him to give me some privacy. He didn't move.

"Do you mind?"

"Yeah, no worries," he said, as he turned to leave. "But make sure to give me back my T-shirt. My girlfriend got it for me."

This was next-level pettiness. This jerk makes breakfast in his bougie name-brand cotton-blend pyjama set, offering me bacon that I can't eat because we both know girls don't chomp on greasy foods in front of fuck buddies. Then he kicks me out while I'm in a shirt that his *girlfriend* bought him—all because he didn't hold up his end of the agreement to take me home.

All I had was my last thread of self-esteem, and all I wanted to do was go home and eat a five-egg omelette to soothe my grumbling stomach—but I had to walk out of his condo first.

I finished dressing, then put my knee-high boots back on in silence. Anthony suggested that I wait in the lobby.

"Do you want me to wait downstairs with you?"

"No, it's okay," I said, thinking maybe he did have a heart.

He smirked. "Good, because I wasn't going to."

For a moment I thought about trashing his place and eating all his bacon. Instead, I click-clacked my way down the hall, into the elevator, and down to the lobby. As the elevator dinged, signalling that I had reached the ground floor with its pristine marble and gold-accented decor, I shivered. I remembered that I had given my jacket to Taz.

My stomach sunk with each new revelation: Black girl with no jacket. Exposed in her 2 a.m. bar outfit at 9:45 on a late-fall morning. In a middle-class white-people building. Far from home. Oh. My. God.

I reluctantly stepped out of the elevator in my high boots, looking around for any sign of life and hoping it would die immediately instead of anyone seeing me like this. The lobby was surrounded by huge glass windows and the sun was pelting my body, which I took as a sign that God was either trying desperately to redeem me or testing me to see if I would burst into flames. I apologized to Him for my un-Catholic, premarital frolics, promising I'd make better choices next time if he just turned me into ash.

I walked slowly towards an expensive beige sofa, trying to silence the clicking from my heels, and plopped down. I looked straight up, right into the security camera pointed towards me. Behind me was the open door where the guard was probably watching. I quickly pulled out my phone and called my favourite cab company.

"Yes, hi. I need a cab," I whispered as I gave him the address.

"We're having a bit of a delay this morning, your cab will arrive in approximately thirty minutes."

"WHAT?"

"Thirty minutes, ma'am."

"Okay, fine. Just please tell him to hurry up."

"Will do, ma'am."

"Like, really hurry—"

Click.

To ease my racing thoughts, I tried to focus on something else, choosing the vase full of fake flowers and beige pebbles. I figured this low and desperate moment in my life would somehow make me eligible for Matilda-like superpowers, so I practised on the vase, chanting at it to tip over, hoping this would be enough to distract any cougars, trophy wives, or soccer moms who came through the lobby.

Ten minutes had passed and no one had come by. Just as I began thinking I could get through this, I heard the elevator doors open.

No.

A woman and her two young daughters emerged, talking cheerfully. I tried to hide myself, make myself compact, but I quickly learned it's quite hard to hide a hoe in an empty lobby. Then another tidbit of knowledge came back to me: Anthony was one of the very few young guys in the building, making this encounter even more painful. *Well, would you look at that, Joanne! Anthony has a mild case of Jungle Fever!*

Their talking died down as soon as they saw me. I looked over and the youngest girl, no more than seven, was staring at me blankly with her finger in her mouth. I felt bad, thinking that I may have just afforded this child her first traumatic memory. The mother looked at me for a moment, wide-eyed, mouth open, clearly disturbed, so I smiled at her.

What else was I supposed to do? I hoped she'd take pity on me, or at least feel nostalgic about her university days. Instead, she put a hand on each of her daughters' shoulders, her eyes still on me.

"Honey, take the keys and meet me by the car," she whispered to the eldest, and pushed them towards the door.

I was mortified. It was more than just being caught in last night's sexy outfit. The look on their faces had shrunk me into nothing. I was out of place on the creaseless beige couch, between the cream walls, among the white people with their perfect clothes in their expensive condos.

Where men have the privilege of fucking without repercussions, women are always crucified for wanting sex. For women of colour, this relationship is complicated by deeply entrenched stereotypes about our sexuality. For centuries, Black women have been called Jezebels, freaks, and Hottentots; we've been labelled primitive, always ready for sex, and always willing to give it.

White women have long been expected to adhere and aspire to the cult of domesticity, the ultimate "true" womanhood—piety, submission, and purity—whereas Black women are considered inherently and irredeemably incapable of possessing these qualities. Instead, Black women face what Black feminist scholar Patricia Hill Collins calls "controlling images": stereotypes and tropes that contribute to the sexual objectification that seeks to keep us oppressed.

In her 1990 holy grail, *Black Feminist Thought: Knowledge, Consciousness, and the Politics of Empowerment*, Collins says these controlling images are always changing and adapting, each becoming a new starting point for a cultural moment that creates new forms of oppression and commercialization. In other words, the names may change as we evolve—Ratchet, Thots, Bad Bitches—but they are still rooted in the same oppressive, damaging narratives about Black women's sexuality.

As casual-sex and hookup culture becomes more prevalent—and the images associated with Black women change in name but continue to be reinforced—it becomes harder for Black women to reclaim their sexuality. Women are demonized for wanting sex; for a Black woman, who is already dealing with stereotypes about her animalistic, insatiable sexuality, it is almost impossible for her to say she likes sex without facing judgement and slut-shaming.

These damaging images have become normalized in our culture and are commonplace: *Is it true that Black women are good in bed? I've never had sex with a Black woman—can you be my first? Once you go Black, you never go back!* It can make it hard to find and have a respectful sexual relationship—or any relationship at all—that isn't tainted by the idea of a Black woman's uncontrollable sexuality and how someone can benefit.

To be a Black woman today means to live in constant hyperawareness of your body. There are voyeuristic eyes on us at all times, objectifying us into parts—ass, pussy, breasts. When we date non-Black people, we know that we, not our partners, are sexualized. We know the sexual connotations of the word *interracial*. We battle with the myth that our bodies are dirty, raunchy, deviant, animalistic, ungodly.

I used to see girls walk home barefoot on London's main road at 8 a.m., holding their vodka-covered stilettos in one hand and using the other to keep their dress from riding up. Guys wandered the streets with dishevelled hair and undone dress shirts and no clue where they were. Walk-of-shamers were as common as morning joggers.

Students—old enough in the public psyche to be sexually active, yet young enough to be messy, hedonistic wrongdoers—get a pass to publicly express sexuality for four years. And this has afforded young women more freedom to take charge of their sex lives. Running back home at dawn with a ripped shirt or a broken stiletto heel is a time-restricted, socially accepted norm for white students.

To do the walk of shame as a Black woman is to confront stereotypes about our sexuality head on, using the same tools and words that oppress us. It's reclaiming the right to celebrate our sexuality in public. It's releasing ourselves from the bonds that have kept us shackled and oppressed in our communities, in society, and within ourselves.

In recent years, young women have used the power of collective walking to take back their right to have consensual sex—and celebrate it. Take Back the Night, which started in the 1970s, has grown into an international event on a mission to end sexual and partner violence. SlutWalk began in 2011 after a Toronto police officer told female students at a safety forum at York University that they shouldn't dress like sluts if they wanted to avoid sexual assault. It is now a global movement in over two hundred cities and over forty countries.

For years, Black feminists in the U.S. have argued that SlutWalk excludes Black women. Amber Rose started her own SlutWalk several years ago as a response to slut-shaming from both tabloids and her exes, Wiz Khalifa and Kanye West. Rose's movement has made space for Black women to condemn sexual injustice and victim-blaming, while also promoting sex positivity and highlighting the unique challenges that we face.

Sexual liberation is different for us. From the late '90s, white women could look up to their *Sex and the City* idols, who iconically scandalized television with the idea that women could have sex like men—and the next generation of white girls followed in the footsteps of characters from its successor, *Girls*. For young women of colour, however, it's more complicated. Who do Black girls have to look up to on the screen? Where are our brunch-table conversations about vibrators and orgasms and sex and love?

Few shows and films have given us accurate, contemporary representations of Black womanhood that are unapologetically sexual. In recent years, we've been graced with Olivia Pope, Annalise Keating, Nola Darling, and the ladies of *Girls Trip*—but other portrayals are still stigmatizing, and few films and TV shows like this had been made when I was at university. Even reality TV shows like *Basketball Wives*, *Real Housewives of Atlanta*, and *Love & Hip Hop* craft images of oversexed Black women who are gold-diggers, freaks, or baby-makers, unable to have healthy and faithful friendships and relationships. Some hip-hop artists still brand any sex-loving Black woman as a thot, hoe, or chickenhead.

Movies continue to portray Black women as sexual deviants undeserving of love, and if we do attempt to explore our sexuality, we are punished by losing everything. In Tyler Perry's *Temptations: Confessions of a Marriage Counselor*, lead character Judith cheats on her husband and is punished by getting HIV. She grows old alone while her husband gets happily remarried to a younger woman. (Perry has a history of playing into negative, punishing stereotypes of Black women in his films.)

I knew the racist constructions of Black female sexuality were impositions of society, and yet I still felt so ashamed of myself sitting on that couch. I wanted to be like other women, to hook up and not worry about the additional stigma, to have sex like men do, to own my sexuality. But that morning, being judged by that woman in that fancy condo building, I felt like a cavity of darkness.

The mother continued to look at me, her mouth slightly parted, seemingly conflicted as her eyes darted between me and the door, and then she left to catch up with her kids.

Twenty minutes later, I saw my cab driving towards the entrance. I flew off the couch and quickly ran outside, taking a nosedive into the backseat.

"Oh my God, thank you so much for coming," I said, as if he had a choice.

"You're welcome, I apologize for the wait—"

"It's okay," I said as I put my seatbelt on. "You're here now."

I sighed with relief and slouched in the seat, savouring the unthreatening silence.

"So, how was it?"

I lifted my head, and paused, giving him a minute to retract his intrusive comment. But at this point my dignity was running on empty, and this cab driver was asking me a question I needed to answer for myself.

"It was good, until it wasn't."

As he drove back into Richmond Row, he gave me a list of reasons why a girl like me, whatever that meant, shouldn't be doing the walk of shame, especially for white boys. I pretended to listen as familiar buildings—Jack's, Barney's, St. Joseph's Hospital—passed by. With each new quarter on the meter, I felt more relieved.

By the time I reached home, it was 11 a.m. People who hadn't embarrassed themselves last night were jogging, and hungover groups of friends were stumbling out of their homes for brunch, to eat and watch the girls run home in their body-con dresses. I paid my driver, thanked him for the ride (not the advice), and went inside. I made myself that five-egg omelette, took a shower, and crawled into my bed.

Act Five

CHORUS: *We called in Tyra Banks in for a favour. [Cuts to Tyra]: I was rooting for you! WE WERE ALL ROOTING FOR YOU!!!!!!!!*

The next time I went to Anthony's condo, it was snowing terribly. An eerie haze illuminated the empty city, the snow on the ground was untouched.

He smoothed out the creases in the teal Egyptian cotton sheets his girlfriend had bought him. I ran my hand over them; it was a thoughtful gift, the kind that showed she was practical and nurturing. I felt that I was neither of these things.

I had refused to feel ashamed about this affair; it was his problem, not mine. But it was finally getting to me—her sheets, the two picture frames on the dresser he purposely put face down when I came over. As I lay beside him, he called his girlfriend and spoke to her so sweetly that I was jealous. After he hung up, he turned over to look at me. I didn't challenge him back with my eyes.

"Can I ask you a question?" he said.

"No."

"Why are you still with me? I thought you would have told me to fuck off by now."

I paused.

"I don't know."

But I did, and it was embarrassing that even he knew I was better than this. When he was playing with my hair, making me laugh, kissing me goodbye, I thought that maybe being cruel was a way to hide how he really felt. I thought I just needed to try harder to help him past his own hesitancy about our relationship.

"What do you see in me that you're still here?" I asked him, trying to deflect from my own bad choices.

"Honestly, I really like Black girls," he said coolly, now laying on his back, his hands behind his head.

"So why do you have a white girlfriend, then?"

"Well, she's really nice, she has a good job, and my parents love her," he said. "I don't want to ruin a good thing."

"So it's just for show?"

"I'm really attracted to Black girls," he said again. "But I could never marry one."

His girlfriend was kind, smart, educated, a hit with his family—things, it seemed, he didn't think were possible for Black women. He talked about the expectation to get married and have kids. "Oh God, E, I hope you don't get pregnant. I hope it's not with me," he said, laughing. "My nonna would flip her shit. She'd say, *Tony, why is your baby Black?*"

Anthony said that he had always wanted to sleep with a Black girl, and he had been trying for years. The closest he'd got was when he actively pursued a maid who cleaned his room at a Cuban resort. "Thanks for being my first," he laughed, then turned over to check his phone.

I heard these comments from men often in bars. But they were unprovoked strangers who were drunk. Said in passing, but still offensive. I didn't want to believe that Anthony was like them, but in this moment, my concerns about our racial differences—the ones that had made me reluctant in the beginning—started to resurface.

"I should go home now," I said, getting up to grab my belongings.

I stared at the backs of the frames, trying to see through them, desperate to see what she looked like, how different we were.

"I'll call you a cab," he said quietly, as he came over and quickly slipped the frames into the top drawer. But he forgot about the one hanging in the hallway. It was a large framed photo of Anthony's family standing in front of a Christmas tree, his girlfriend's hand on his chest, both of them smiling. She was thin with short brown hair, big brown eyes, and flushed cheeks, like his. They looked so happy. He kissed me goodbye in front of the photo. Wedged between his perfect life and a lie, I promised myself I would never come back.

Act Six

CHORUS: *We've renamed you Oscar Martis because this man is trash and you apparently like living in a garbage can. Why do you keep going back?! We can't with your sad and sorry ass.*

It had been a week since I last saw Anthony, and it was the first weekend that he didn't text me. His girlfriend was in town.

Instead of ruining Taz's night, I decided to stay in and be miserable about my life decisions with my laptop and a mountain of snacks. As any bored person does on a Saturday night indoors, I creeped.

I tried to remember Anthony's Twitter handle from a night when he'd shown me his profile. He said it was mainly full of him tweeting his favourite rap lyrics. "Don't add me though," he told me, laughing.

Two hours of amateur sleuthing later, I found his account.

Hmm . . . he really likes the word nigga.

Wow, he's talking to a Black woman? Oh, he's talking to a few Black women. He's been talking to them since we started hooking up.

Anthony's Twitter page was full of interactions with Black women. He had just messaged a girl a few hours ago. Most of the messages were platonic, discussing music and radio shows, like the texts he had sent me when we'd first met. Others seemed obsessive. He was following a dozen Black female porn stars. Like a fanboy, he fawned over them, sending them his number, asking them to message back.

I'm a big fan.

Here's my number, give me a call.

Let's meet up, I would love to take you out for breakfast.

A feeling of disgust—of complete violation—moved through me, bringing me to tears.

He was obsessed with the myth of Black female sexuality. He was turned on by the parts of our bodies, the secrets of pleasure we held between our legs. And I was the lab rat he experimented on.

When he told me about liking Black girls, and me being his "first," I hadn't thought he was actively searching for us. But I had become a body with which he could play out his sexual fantasies, to build enough confidence to find other Black girls he could add to his hit list.

I cried myself to sleep that night and for nights after. It didn't matter how much I showered, my body felt dirty and used.

I walked around campus in a daze. Meanwhile, Anthony, oblivious to my breakdown, was texting me again.

Taz commiserated, but she didn't understand the extent of my reaction. I didn't understand it either, it was as if my body had known there was an intruder and shut down on itself. I couldn't describe the detachment, the disgust I felt for this contaminated shell.

I thought I knew what an assault on my body felt like. I had experienced deliberate, textbook physical attacks. But this was something else. Anthony had violated me without force. It was a different kind of power and control, but still a taking. And this had made my own body foreign to me, a shameful burden. I hated this problem with no name, this invasion that I knew I'd never recover from.

My hurt had turned into anger. He had stolen something from me—broken my trust. He needed to be reminded of who I was, of what he would miss, before I walked away for good. I wanted to make him feel terrible for how he'd treated me, and I wanted to see his regret in person.

I went to his apartment one last time in the New Year, burning with shame but with nothing to lose. And when I saw his face—exhausted, his eyes distant, embarrassed—I realized that he absolutely hated himself. And in hating himself, he hated me too. I was a scapegoat for his weakness, his guilt over wanting women who looked like me, women he was raised not to desire. And I was relying on our moments of tenderness to once again prove that I could be with someone, despite them being unsure about me. "Take me home. Right now," I said.

He nodded. "I'll get the keys."

The ride back in his rusty Honda Civic was extremely quiet. He apologized for the mess, throwing newspapers and old Starbucks coffee cups onto the backseat. I told him it didn't matter and sat on them, my legs bare under my peacoat.

He looked over. "Are you cold? I'll get you my jacket."

He shuffled around the back of the car as I protested. I didn't want his fickle chivalry now. Still, he wrapped it around my legs and turned the heat up.

We drove in silence until he approached my street. I knew we only had minutes left with each other. "If you're so unhappy with your life, then why don't you just change it?" I asked.

"I don't know," he replied. "I wish I could be like you. You're courageous and optimistic. You just love your life. But I don't know." It got quiet again. "I'm sorry I'm such an asshole," he said, looking straight ahead, swallowing silently.

"It's okay."

"You're a good kid."

When he pulled into my driveway, the air thickened. Dawn was breaking. He parked the car and we sat in silence for a few minutes, the only sound the gentle chirping of birds.

There was no kiss goodbye, no words. I got out of the car, walked up the steps, and went to my room. I took off my clothes, got into bed, and cried myself to sleep.

CHORUS: *And she wins the Academy Award for Best Performance for the Most Dramatic, Unnecessary Choices That Make Life Hella Difficult for No Reason (she is currently available to star in a lead role in any Issa Rae production!).*

Epilogue

CHORUS: *Shit, there's more! [Pulls bag of popcorn onto lap, starts munching.]*

My period was late.

Not "three days" kind of late. It was over two weeks late. Pregnancy-scare kind of late.

The day after ending things with Anthony, I got bronchitis and couldn't get out of bed. It was like my body was trying to punish me. It ached like I'd been in the boxing ring, and I had a nasty bout of nausea and a heightened sense of smell that seemed to last for days.

And, my period was late.

Not only had I not been able to shake the feeling that one gets from being used as a racial novelty for the sexual pleasure of a white guy, I was now horrified that I was carrying his child. There were no Yahoo answers to help with this dilemma.

All I could think about was what he'd said about babies: *My nonna would flip her shit. She'd say, Tony, why is your baby Black?*

He would be ashamed; hooking up with a Black girl could be hidden within the walls of his bedroom. But a biracial baby? That was a mistake everyone could see.

I tried to think of ways to make the little embryo unstick itself from my uterine wall. I tried falling down the stairs like Drew Barrymore's character in *Riding in Cars with Boys*, but I lost my nerve and slinked all the way down to the last step. I looked up ways to induce your period, which included eating copious amounts of parsley or shoving it up your vagina, but that seemed like the start of another problem rather than a solution.

I needed a pregnancy test, but I was too broke to buy one. In an attempt to rid me of my sadness, Taz dragged me to the bar so I could sulk in public instead. As I was walking to the washroom to check if my period had arrived, I found $10 in loose bills and change scattered across the floor of the stall. Then I found another $4 in loonies by the counter.

The next evening after class, Taz and I walked to the drug store up the street to buy the test.

Beside a sale sticker was a no-name brand test for $10.88. I was tired and scared that I was carrying the spawn of a race-chaser, so I whined about how I wanted the name-brand test, a whopping $22, because it claimed to detect pregnancy sooner and I really needed this whole chapter of my life to be over ASAP.

After I threw my childish fit in the family-planning aisle, we took the no-name test to the checkout to stand in an unacceptably long line. Only one cash was open, manned by an older woman with a Kate Gosselin haircut who looked like her name was Deborah. She moved extremely slowly, like she wanted to stay late at work, and the line behind us grew right into one of the aisles.

When it was our turn, I placed the pregnancy test on the counter face down.

Deborah scanned my test and put it upright, making me wince in humiliation.

"Your total is $18.76," she said, loudly.

"No," I said, leaning over the counter in a hushed voice. "It's supposed to be on sale for $10.88. There's a big sticker."

She looked unimpressed.

"Ma'am, it's coming up as $18.76," she said. We engaged in a stare-off.

"Can you call someone, please, to get a price check?"

Deadpan Deb slowly picked up the phone and hit the PA button. It beeped. "Could I get a price check on a pregnancy test?" Her voice was a crackled echo through the store. The entire line, about twelve people, was listening.

Another old white lady came to the front to collect the test.

"The brand-name test was on sale," she called from the aisle. "It's all sold out."

"Is there another pregnancy test that I can give these ladies for a similar price?" Deb yelled back.

"No, there's no other pregnancy tests here for cheap!"

"You know what? You've been very helpful, but we'll just take the first one we had," Taz said, sensing I was about to explode.

Deb got back on the PA. "Can you please bring back the no-name pregnancy test?"

I was sweating as I counted out the bills and change that I'd found last night on the bar floor. Deborah collected them slowly as my test lay there, the box once again upright and facing every-one in the line, who all looked quite invested in my misfortune.

She handed me the receipt. My test was still standing there for all to see.

"Can I have a bag?" I was bewildered.

"It's five cents."

Taz quickly grabbed the box off the counter and dragged me out before I unleashed hormonal fury on Deborah.

When we got home, I took the test. There was one line—not pregnant.

The next day, I got my period.

///

A year later, I still hadn't made sense of my relationship with Anthony, or my own emotions about his Black-girl fetish.

I also hadn't forgiven myself for getting into that mess, and I'd come to an understanding that my relationship to my body would never be the same. It felt marked and unfamiliar, something I didn't recognize in the mirror—although nothing had really changed. That feeling didn't go away, even as I started dating someone new. I didn't know how to explain what I was going through to him, or my friends. Their problems seemed simple: their boyfriends sucked, they were jerks. There was no explaining that I had been on someone's racial Fuck Bucket List. I walked around with this heavy shame, a problem with no solution.

During a Women's Studies class a year after our break up, we were assigned bell hooks's essay "Eating the Other: Desire and Resistance." As I devoured the piece, relief moved through my body. I nearly shot out of my seat, taking out my highlighter and marking up every page. It was the first time I felt relief in a year.

In the essay, hooks describes a moment walking behind a group of white jock-type boys in downtown New Haven, near the Yale campus where she taught. She overhears them talking about how they want to sleep with as many women from various racial and ethnic groups as possible before they graduate. hooks breaks down their ranking system: Asian girls are the easiest to catch, Indigenous girls much harder to find. Black women rank high on the list of sexual conquests:

> To these young males and their buddies, fucking was a way to confront the Other, as well as a way to make themselves over, to leave behind white "innocence" and enter the world of "experience." As is often the case in this society, they were confident that non-white people had more life experience, were more worldly, sensual, and sexual because they were different. Getting a bit of the Other, in this case engaging in sexual encounters with non-white females, was considered a ritual of transcendence, a movement out into a world of difference that would transform, an acceptable rite of passage. The

direct objective was not simply to sexually possess the Other; it was to be changed in some way by the encounter. "Naturally," the presence of the Other, the body of the Other, was seen as existing to serve the ends of white male desires.

Through sleeping with a woman of colour, hooks argues, white men believe they gain access to dark, otherworldly territory, transcending their whiteness and innocence and moving into more sexually experienced and dangerous terrain. The man who does this believes that the body of this non-white Other holds the most delectable pleasures, a tale to share with his friends, and a checkmark on his list.

But, hooks says, after "consuming" her multiple times, he becomes bored with his ethnic conquest and spits her out—moving on to the next one.

It was as if hooks had been in my head. What I couldn't articulate was there, on paper, immortalized as a theory. And that meant what I was feeling wasn't made up.

Feminist theory is all about theory, and praxis—enacting that theory. hooks's work, as well as the writings of many feminist scholars I was reading in my Women's Studies courses, made it easy to write about Anthony using already-established theories, through documented experiences. I realized my own were already part of a legacy of these stories.

I wrote an article for an acquaintance's blog—tying in hooks's analysis and my relationship with Anthony and other men I'd come across in London. The next morning, an editor at the *Huffington Post* contacted me to ask if they could run it on their website. It was my first published piece. It went viral, sparking heated debates.

Dozens of people sent me messages, thankful to see their experiences reflected in a mainstream publication. They used the article to start having long-overdue conversations with the people in their lives about race and relationships. People of colour from around the world shared their experiences of being fetishized, while others reflected on how they had exotified past partners.

And so my unconventional Greek tragedy goes, except nobody poked their own eyes out or accidentally killed their father and married their mother. Anthony and his girlfriend broke up a year or so later. He is now married to a woman of colour and has a child.

I still haven't gone out with another white guy. But I'm open to it—I do love me some Patrick Wilson and white boys in cardigans. While I don't get many sexually racist messages anymore, I don't get approached by white guys either. It will still take some work to open up again, for someone new to gain my trust and vulnerability.

And that is the real tragedy—the way the body remembers past lovers, the way it seizes at a scent or a memory. How it can pack itself up in a flash at the reminder of them, leaving nothing but impenetrable, impossible borders for the next person to try to cross.

The Token in the Residence Bathroom

WHAT TO EXPECT: Quite possibly the most stressful part of the communal dorm experience and a coordinated effort. You will be at the mercy of a bunch of catty, shit-analyzing people who have nothing better to do than try to figure out everyone's fecal sights and smells like it's a murder mystery. As a minority, you will break into a cold sweat every time you need to do a number two. You will study everyone's bathroom habits to know exactly who goes when and in what stalls, because if it's ill-timed, they will see your little brown toes planted on the ground and you will get a shit nickname (literally, a shit nickname) like Vegan Shits or Bitch With Floaters. I don't want this for you.

HOW TO DEAL WITH IT: Using this four-pronged approach, you will never get caught taking a shit as yourself again. All you need is another person with a similar skin tone.

> **1. Blame the other person.** If your nosy shithound floormates are having their daily shit talk, and on the agenda is an unidentified poop that belongs to you, just point the finger at the other person of colour. Tell them you saw OBP (Other Brown/Black Person) running to the bathroom in a hurry this morning. The case of who smelt it dealt it doesn't apply here— save yourself, you need this.
>
> **2. Steal their identity.** Most people in residence leave their doors wide open. Take advantage and swipe the other person's slippers in case anyone is brazen enough to look under the stall. You can also lift your legs up

and press them against the stall door (ghost shits)—
this way you can confuse and disarm Shitlock Holmes
by making them think that there's a Moaning Myrtle
situation happening up in there.

3. Use their nail polish. If some people say they
can't tell minorities apart then you can be damn sure
our toes all look the same too! Observe the painted
toenails of the other person of colour. Comment on
how great their nail polish is and ask if you can borrow
it. They will most likely say yes (if not, go buy one that
looks similar). Paint your toenails with their polish and
go to town.

4. Wear their pants. Okay—extreme, I know. But
depending on how dire your situation is and your level
of friendship, wear their bottoms (lounge pants are
roomier) to the porcelain throne. Return what you
take as soon as you can—you're not a damn crook.

relationshit

If they were to ever have a baby, my father said to my mother, he didn't want a Gemini.

Years later, on Thanksgiving Day, she stood in the living room as she told her parents that she was twenty-two and pregnant—the only person in our family to have a baby out of wedlock. She was due June 23—a Cancer, two days out of Gemini territory. From the beginning of her pregnancy, family members and strangers predicted she was having a boy—from the way she was carrying, the changing shape of her nose, and their own symbolic dreams. As she prepared for life with her Cancer son, something else happened: I arrived one month early, in the middle of May, a Gemini. Even my arrival was dramatic and spiteful, our key traits.

My mother was young, and with me being their only grandchild, my grandparents willingly became my primary caretakers. They showered me in affection, took me travelling around the world, and enrolled me in every extracurricular activity imaginable. Still, my grandfather was disappointed; he'd wanted my mom to establish herself before having a child. But he was adamant that she not give into pressure to get married just because she had a baby.

My mom called off her engagement when I was six months old and, following an easy court win, she was granted sole custody, and my father was given visitation. He rarely used it. He's in and out of our family albums, mostly before I was born—photographed with his arm draped around my mother before she was pregnant, or sitting comfortably on our couch with his feet up, or posing at family events. There are a few photos with me: a close-up of him cradling me as a newborn; the two of us on a family vacation to Disney World when I was eight months old; me sitting on his lap during my first Christmas. In other photos, he's been scratched out with scissors.

When he did show up to school events or dance recitals, I felt proud to show the other kids that I had a father just like they did. But his presence made me uneasy. The way he smelled like car cleaner. How he chewed mint gum. His silver tooth filling. A smiling face that always seemed to betray his fickleness. I despised how he could disappear for months and then show up like he had done nothing wrong. When my grandmother was battling cancer, he didn't come around to thank the woman who had raised his child. When she died, he didn't come around to comfort me, or help care for me. He didn't come around at all.

I haven't seen my father in a decade. Before that, it was six years. Before that, five. Each time he makes his grand appearance, he sticks around longer. Each time he decides to leave, his time away becomes greater. My grandfather refers to him as "your father" before shaking his head in disappointment, though he'll never utter an unkind word. My mother and I give him nicknames—Mr. Worldwide, Mr. International, Sperm Donor. It makes him easier to talk about.

Most of what I know about my father is superficial, things that I've seen during our brief periods of contact, or that my mother sees in me: his oily skin, his wide nose, his long legs and short torso, his love for carrot cake, the way his eyes turn into crinkled slits when he smiles. I hope that I haven't inherited his temper, his lack of commitment, his selfishness. If she's noticed anything else, she hasn't mentioned it. I pray that she doesn't.

///

The moment I learned that my father had other children was captured on camera.

I was twelve, and finally old enough to be home alone while my mom went out. I had been wanting to find my father for some time, starved for pieces of information about his life that she wouldn't give. I hadn't seen him in several years, not since my grandmother was alive. I went searching through the family phone book, a beaten-up heirloom from the Chinese market with a red, decorative cover, containing phone numbers inscribed from before I was born. As I flipped through the thinning pages, I found his name in my grandmother's writing. I started to cry, overwhelmed by happiness and fear. What would I say? Would he recognize the voice of his own child? I rehearsed how our conversation would go, and an hour later, when I finally called, he didn't answer. I left a voicemail—this was Eternity, his daughter. Did he remember me? I was looking for him. Could he call me back, please?

He didn't call back that day, or the next. I left him several messages. Finally, on the car ride to school the following week, my mom gently asked if I had been trying to get in touch with my father. Heat rose to my face.

"Yes," I said defiantly as I thrust my chin up to knock back the sting of embarrassed tears. "And you can't stop me."

"I'm not trying to stop you at all," she said. Her empathetic tone made me angrier; I thought she was pitying me. "You can have a relationship with him, but I just don't want you to get your hopes up."

"He's my dad," I said, with a little less conviction.

"I'm just saying that he's known where you've lived for the last twelve years, that's all."

She didn't say anything more, and neither did I.

A week after the conversation with my mom, we went to his mother's house, where he lived, for our reunion.

My mother and I got into the shaky elevator and entered the off-white hallway that smelled like cooked food and onions. I made my mother knock on the door. My grandmother, a small and fragile Black woman, answered.

"Oh, Eternity! How are you? Come hug Grandma!" I hugged her back to be polite. My father wasn't home yet, so she gave us a tour of the apartment, a cluttered unit with parquet floors, beige walls, and brown furniture.

It was daytime but the brown suede curtains were fully closed. A small crack of light had managed to get through. In its rays were dust particles. I looked around cautiously. I wasn't familiar with the reality of public housing. It lacked the space and the warmth of the home I lived in with my grandparents. I immediately regretted my choice to seek out this new family.

The living room was piled high with junk—on tabletops, on side tables, in the glass cabinet. The only place that wasn't covered in fake shrubberies and trinkets was one side of the couch. The dining room table was barely visible under dozens of fake plants, all potted and perfectly lined up in rows. "Try one," my grandmother said to me, ushering me to push a button on one of the dusty dancing plants, its plastic leaves laced with cobwebs. I reluctantly pressed the tiny red button on the pot and the flower bobbed and played an upbeat jazz tune, its stiff leaves moving up and down.

"Do you like it?" she asked.

"Um. Yes?" I hated it. It was awful and ugly. She plucked it from the table and put it in my hands, her eyes glimmering. "You can have it."

As the flower continued to dance in my hands, my grandmother ran into the kitchen to get her Polaroid camera.

"Come, I want to take your picture," she said, and I followed her back into the hall.

"Stand there." She pointed to the middle of the hallway and shaped me into an acceptable pose, like a life-sized doll. I was uncomfortable, fidgeting with my hands until I clasped them in front of me and gave a tight-lipped grin.

It wasn't good enough, not when I had such a beautiful smile, she said—a smile with front teeth starkly divided down the middle thanks to the gap I had inherited from her son. Her compliment worked. The camera went off with a giant flash.

She wanted to take one more for my father. Feeling more comfortable, I gave her a bigger smile. She said something about how happy she was that I was here.

"I have a photo of all of Nicholas's kids in this hallway," she said excitedly.

I thought I'd heard her incorrectly. I struggled to keep some semblance of a smile on my face as my lips shook. I squeezed my hands together tightly, folding my arms in, making myself small, to pretend I could just disappear. The camera flashed again.

"Come, girl. Come see." She pulled the photo out from the bottom of the camera, waving it back and forth. "You look just like Krystal," she said.

She brought me back inside the apartment and into the kitchen, returning with a tin box containing several other Polaroid pictures. She pulled one out. It was a picture of a young biracial girl. She, too, was standing in the off-white hallway, her hands also clasped together, looking slightly uncomfortable. My grandmother told me that was Krystal, my younger sister who lived in England, who visited every couple of years. I'd never heard of her until now.

My grandmother took my now-dried Polaroid and tossed it on top of the stack of other photos of brown-skinned kids in the off-white hallway, before shutting the tin. I remember feeling like part of me was now locked in that box, where she collected us all like baseball cards.

I don't remember seeing my father that day, though he did show up. I do remember that, for a while, we saw each other every week, either going to Harvey's for hotdogs or eating chocolate in front of my house after school in his busted-up red car.

I was about to enter Grade 8. I'd just grown out of being the target of school bullies, and I no longer had to worry about monitoring how I acted and moved through the day to avoid being made fun of by my peers. But now I was self-policing in other ways. When I was with my father, I watched how I ate, the way I responded to his questions, the way I behaved. I didn't want him to find me annoying. I didn't want him to leave me again.

During one of our evenings out, my father bought a bag of Oh Henry! Bites and I ate nearly all of them. I expected him to be disgusted at my gluttony, but instead he laughed. The next time he picked me up, he wanted to get me my own. He drove to a strip mall drugstore near the home he shared with my grandmother, and parked the car right in front. I begged him to let me come in with him. My mother would never leave me in the car alone in a strange place. But he dismissed my fear, promising he would only be a minute. I was a big girl, right? He'd even put on the radio for me. But I was scared to be in this unfamiliar neighbourhood. Plus, I wanted to go *with* him, be in public with my dad—be validated as his child. Why couldn't we just go together?

As he walked away, the panic crept in. And when he didn't come back—more than five minutes had passed, maybe ten—I got out of the car and went inside the store, frantically calling his name. But I couldn't find him. I ran back to the car and pulled on the handle, but the door wouldn't budge. I cried hysterically, vulnerable in this unknown place, feeling that I had just become a difficult and emotional daughter who didn't take orders—locked out of his car, locked out of his life. When he finally came back, Bites in his hand, his eyes were wide and his mouth open. He was shocked at how hysterical I was. He said he didn't expect me to act this way. I was devastated, ashamed—and worse, terrified that my actions would scare him off. I didn't bring up how angry I was that he'd left me alone. I remained silent the whole way home, the Bites resting between us, uneaten. Weeks later, after promising to pick me up for dinner, he left me waiting for him on our doorstep. It would be years before he showed up again.

///

My father came back into my life at two pivotal moments: the first had been during that rocky transition into adolescence; the second was six years later, during my collision with womanhood.

Life went on without him, for years. I graduated elementary school, then high school, then I started my first year of university. I made peace with what my mom had said: he knew where to find me. I had no interest in reaching out to my father again.

But I wanted to know my siblings. After that afternoon in his mother's hallway, I searched for Krystal nearly every day without telling anyone. I felt hopeless; she could've been in any city in England, and all I had to go off of was a childhood photo— I didn't even have the spelling of her name. Each day, I typed variations of her name into a search engine, hoping for different results this time. Each night, I thought about our reunion and tried not to lose hope.

Weeks before my first holiday break at Western, I stumbled upon a girl on Facebook whose first name was a shortened version of Krystal. Over the years, I had searched endless profiles, looking for a resemblance to the girl in the photo in the faces of these women. She was the closest match to the girl in the photo. She looked like me.

I sent her a message, asking her if she knew a man by my father's name. She said he was her dad, and I told her that I thought we were sisters. Krystal didn't hesitate; she knew who I was. She had also been looking for me. I was eighteen when I found my sister.

There was so much about Krystal I had missed out on, and there's much I still don't know. She is nine months younger than me. She's lived in a small town in the United Kingdom for so long that she has a thick English accent. She's a professional athlete. Though she lives across the ocean, she is still suffering the immense pain of feeling abandoned by our father. Unlike me, she hasn't given up trying to reach out to him. We stay connected through social media, congratulating each other on our achievements and liking each other's posts. We send the occasional message to remind one another that we love each other immensely, even if we haven't met.

Three months after I connected with Krystal, I was home for the weekend when the doorbell rang. Jehovah's Witnesses were making their rounds in the neighbourhood this time of year, and my mother went downstairs to answer. Her voice was low, hushed. When she came back upstairs, she was sullen and pained.

"There's someone here to see you." I didn't recognize the seriousness in her voice, or her disturbed expression. My mother was a jokester, always in good spirits even when she was upset or hurting. I went downstairs. It took many seconds to recognize my father's face.

"What do you want?" Those were the only words that offered to come out—the only appropriate response.

He stared at me in awe, almost on the verge of tears. "You are so beautiful. You're so big now."

"What did you want?"

"To see you," he said weakly like even he knew the answer was not so simple.

I hesitated, but I let him come upstairs, and we spoke for half an hour. He asked me to give him another chance to make it right. I didn't want to open that part of myself up again. But I pitied him, how desperate he was, how clueless he was about me. He pulled a scraggly piece of paper out of his pocket with a number and a name: *Simone*. It was the contact information for my older sister, he said, and she wanted to meet me.

When I got back to London after winter break, my father, as promised, contacted me. He'd call during class, or in the evenings. He tried to force his way back into my life, pestering me about calling him "Dad," refusing to hang up until I said "I love you." Not wanting to hurt or embarrass him, I forced it out with such difficulty that it made me physically sick. I stayed silent while he tried to guess my favourite colour, my favourite food, my age. He gushed about Simone, but he never brought up any of his other kids. He never admitted to or apologized for his absence in any of our lives.

The uneasiness that I felt about him had resurfaced: a pit in the bottom of my stomach, a cold sweat, a lingering tension and anxiety made worse by hearing his voice. His intrusion in my life drained me. The burden of deciding whether I could make peace with his disruptive presence or if I should confront him about his absence made it hard to focus on anything else. I hoped his interest in me would fizzle out again as it always had before, and that things would go back to the way they were. But I didn't want to come off as cold-hearted or ungrateful—what kind of child calls their father to ask him to leave them alone? While friends socialized in each other's rooms, I retreated to my own, thinking about him, my newfound siblings, and this whole other life that ran parallel to mine—an alternate life that I could have been living but couldn't even imagine for myself—all on top of the new life I was already trying to build.

A month later, Simone called me. "Hey, sis." It was the first time I had ever heard her voice. "I know we haven't met but I'm your big sister and I love you," she said. "And you're the first person I'm telling this to, but . . . I'm pregnant. You're going to be an aunt!"

We spoke as if the circumstances had not robbed us of the chance to know each other. Simone said she had known about me since she was a child. We had lived our lives only thirty minutes away from each other, always close but with no chance of connecting. Simone said I had more nieces—children of her older brother—and that we had even more siblings: Devin was the oldest, followed by Simone. Then there was me, Krystal, Andre—Simone and Devin's full brother—two younger boys, and a baby who Simone didn't know well; there were too many to keep track of, and possibly more. Our father was in and out of their lives.

I never thought I'd have the privilege of having a niece. With no siblings, no close cousins or family outside of my mother and grandfather, I had come to terms with not being an aunt. To hear Simone place me in this role without even knowing me, entrusting me with this title, was an honour.

I was overjoyed for her—for us—but I mourned the years of our lost connection. I didn't know what it meant to be a sister, let alone an aunt.

Finding Simone was the only valuable part of seeing my father again. We have so much in common—an interest in astrology (she's an Aries, like our father), shared political views, the same sense of humour, a love of energy healing and spirituality. We meet up when we can, and in the meantime, we text and send each other holiday cards.

My sister's love has kept us close, even when I was so afraid of this life-changing relationship that I pulled away. She sends me photos of my niece. She's come out to support me in my career and has even met my mother, bridging our worlds. I wish I had met her when we were children, before life got busy. I think about the lost time with my niece, who has grown so much every time I get to see her.

When I was twenty-six, Simone invited my mother and me to my niece's seventh birthday. At the candy-themed party, my niece ran around with her friends, her tutu bouncing up and down, her smile of pure joy. I was relieved when she looked at me with that same happiness and familiarity, leaping into my arms, kissing me. But I also felt sadness. Standing against the wall, I watched her interact with Simone's friends like they were family. People sat at round tables chatting and laughing, already well acquainted. I was an insider by DNA, but an outsider in their lives. I thought about how much time it would take, how much effort would be needed to fit in as if I had been there from the beginning, as if we hadn't grown up in two different families. There was no equation I could solve, no calculation to determine that it could happen in this lifetime.

But, despite our lost time, I feel a sense of pride that is new to me, just knowing I have siblings. It is incredible the way my father's adult children all support each other even though we don't know each other well. It is miraculous in itself that we have all grown up to be accomplished, intelligent, loving, protective, and kind. It's as if there's an unspoken agreement that we will never let his genes define who we are.

I like to think of all of my father's kids as seeds of the same wilted flower, scattered across this universe—not doomed by virtue of our breeding but, instead, surviving because we are uplifted by the forceful winds of our strong-willed mothers and the purest beams of sunshine from our rundown grandparents, who selflessly took on the burdens of parenthood again—whose labour is never done. They give up everything to make up for the man who gives nothing. They break themselves just to see us bloom.

///

Through my two sisters, I heard some of the ways in which my father disrespected the mothers of his children—the secretiveness, the cheating, the emotional and physical unavailability. I learned about his own abusiveness towards women not long after my own assault. My father had latched on to the women around him, a parasite—taking advantage of them, hurting them as they loved him, taking away parts of their lives while creating new ones. He had caused enough pain—to my mother, to my family, to my siblings, and to me.

As I thought about how to tell him I wanted to end our relationship, I stopped responding to his calls and replied with one-word answers to his texts. One day in March, he texted me: *Happy Birthday! Your birthday is sometime soon, right?*

I had put off ending my relationship with Joshua because I didn't want to hurt him. I almost paid with my life. Now, my father was costing me what little peace I had left. *No. You're not even close*, I texted back. Then I blocked and deleted my father's number from my phone.

I haven't spoken to him since. When I see Simone, who is in rare contact with him, we both refer to him as her father, not mine.

There is no amount of viscosity in our shared blood that could convince me that I must speak to my father, or that I will inevitably end up like him. His mistakes are not mine to atone for. As I made myself absent from my father's life, I tried to make myself whole again.

I am still trying.

/ / /

In between stuffing our mouths with chocolate and extra-buttery popcorn, Taz and I unleashed our failures into the universe, proclaiming that we had just hit rock bottom, again.

This ritual happened every week on my queen-sized bed, where we usually both slept. Equipped with snacks, our coziest pyjamas, and the TV shows we spent hours streaming on our laptops, we aired the self-inflicted grievances that had us feeling low-down, no good, and triflin': a fuckboy we'd caught feelings for but swore we wouldn't see again; the brownies we'd eaten out of the garbage for the third time that week; the 8 a.m. classes we'd missed so often that the professor didn't recognize us when we finally showed up. After we admitted our guilt to each other, we'd help one another make resolutions to do better—a fresh start.

We wanted to keep ourselves and each other accountable, but playing the role of responsible adult was a hard task. One minute Taz was bribing me with ice cream to just let go of the bathroom rug so I could at least cry hysterically over a guy in the comfort of my bed; the next I was consoling her as she cried for home, mascara-stained tears down her face and a cigarette between her quivering lips. Sometimes we hit rock bottom at the same time: homesick, lonely, and without purpose. We were six feet under and resurrected so many times that we began buying each other greeting cards from the encouragement section, with motivational messages like "Things will get better" and "Good luck on your new journey."

Without any outside guidance, each mistake felt like a defeat. We didn't yet understand that tripping over the fine line between freedom and failure was part of the growing pains of easing into young adulthood on our own, far from home and without parental support.

One place we would go to feel in control was the library. We'd put on a nice outfit, do our makeup, then pack our backpacks to spend hours at the Allyn and Betty Taylor Library—eating pseudo-healthy snacks, trying to study, and scoping out boys who seemed like a better alternative than the guys we'd meet at bars.

After Joshua, I wasn't ready for another serious relationship, but I wanted to start dating again. I knew from movies that the cool girl always got further than the needy girls. I scoured lifestyle magazines and relationship advice columns. I learned about the necessity of the chase. That being chill—not a nag—makes you the one they'll stick around for. (I know now that ideas like these are just patriarchal requirements that tell women that, in order to be desirable to men, in order to be in a relationship, you should not have needs, concerns, or expectations. And if you do, don't express them.) At the time, I thought it would work.

And it did, temporarily.

I didn't meet anyone at the library, but I did date a couple of guys that I met on our nights out. I voiced no issues or complaints in these brief relationships. I waved away their half-hearted guilt with a smile when they didn't call, and shrugged when they cancelled plans. I didn't open my mouth to demand we talk about the status of our relationship or say that I didn't like the way I was treated. I was an almost-girlfriend, a maybe-girlfriend, a conquest, a convenience. I let men walk all over me, and once I finally had enough, I walked out, only to end up doing the same thing in the next relationship. I'd done it with Anthony—even when his disrespect was blatant, I didn't want to make him uncomfortable by bringing it up. I didn't want to look irrational or hysterical.

Women are often socialized to be inconvenienced and not inconvenience. If we speak against this dynamic then we're selfish and demanding. We're trained to be okay with discomfort, especially when the source of that discomfort is men. Meanwhile, men are socialized to go after what they want, whatever the cost to others—including their partners. This is also true in casual relationships, which often begin in a post-secondary setting where hookup culture condones the mistreatment of each other. To have fun and be casual seems to negate basic human dignity.

We prefer to blame women for staying with assholes rather than question men for their actions. And we've seen what happens when we do call out men, especially on social media platforms. Suddenly we're angry, crazy nags. We're ugly, undesirable feminists. We deserve to be raped, harassed, killed. All for asking men to do better.

In my four years of dating in London, I met all kinds of men who became part of my relationship repertoire: cuddle buddies, friends with benefits, "I'll see you at the bar" guys, boyfriends. I navigated these encounters by acting chill and compliant. I often didn't ask men to do better. Even when I was drained from giving undeserved chances, even when I was ashamed of myself for my lenience, saying nothing seemed better than saying anything at all.

///

To find Black people in London, you needed to know where to look. On Mondays and Wednesdays, some Black folk came out for dollar-beer night at Jack's. Then there was Twisted Thursday. If you didn't go to Twisted Thursday, you would never know that so many Black people existed in London. Dozens filled the club and streets in swarms, just to show off and show out. On Fridays, those same people were at Up On Carling. On Saturday, they were at Club Large, a Black-owned nightclub.

Twisted Thursday was a weekly bar night organized by Jamaican international students that took place in the back of the Barking Frog. They played dancehall, reggae, and soca, drawing in the Caribbean crowd from across the city. It was the best-kept secret in town—even bartenders who worked in the main lounge didn't know it existed. It was a small crowd, one that became more familiar with every passing event. There were no white boys pointing and laughing at us when we danced; no one jumping up and down and spilling their drinks on us or pushing past us in a crowd. Here, people knew what it was like to be the outsider in a bar.

Taz and I never missed a Thursday, but the night I met Nathan, I nearly didn't go. We arrived late, and he was standing in my usual spot. All by himself, a cross between Malcolm X and The Weeknd, he was dressed in a long-sleeve, red-and-black plaid flannel shirt and fitted black jeans. He was tall with broad shoulders and brown hair buzzed short. As he texted on his phone, the light illuminated his furrowed brow and his full, pink lips that were parted slightly. When he finally looked up, he smiled at me, and asked if I wanted to dance.

Nathan spun me around and pulled me close. Something about him felt familiar; the rest felt like trouble.

"What's your name?" His voice was surprisingly deep and husky.

"Eternity," I said.

"Eternity." He lifted his hand up to my shoulder and slowly grazed a finger down my arm, leaving behind a trail of goosebumps—his eyes never breaking contact. "That's a name I'll never forget."

Nathan went to college in Hamilton. He was visiting friends in London that weekend. Soon, we were casually seeing each other. He was the first person I had really liked since Anthony. With Nathan, I didn't have to worry about being used as a novelty.

When I visited him, we got to know more about each other. He encouraged my writing, the one skill he said he wished he had. We talked about Drake's latest album, *Take Care*. Nathan rarely cracked a smile, though he was never mean or moody. It made it all the more satisfying when I'd make a joke and, at the most unexpected times, a giggle would emerge from his lips. His dry sense of humour and monotone delivery made me laugh, even when he was being serious. It felt like we had known each other for years: our hands immediately clasped when we walked side by side; my head rested naturally on his shoulder when we went to the movies. I was nursing a crush so intense I could barely speak.

But sometimes, I wouldn't hear from him for weeks. We had never talked about what our relationship was or where it was going, so I hung on to the small wins—a smiley-face emoji, how quickly he texted me back, if he kept the conversation going, when he suggested our next meet-up—reassurance that our relationship wasn't as casual as it seemed.

Just before March Break in my second year, Nathan texted me. *I'm coming up to London for March Break. I'd love to stay with you.*

Yes, of course, I texted back. I gave myself permission to imagine what our beautiful weekend together would look like, and the possibility of a relationship after I confessed my feelings.

But, that Friday, Nathan texted me to say he was in town—and that he was staying with a friend. Did he forget our plans? I tried to ignore my gut instinct that this wasn't going to end up the way I hoped, and solemnly got ready—my hair big and curly, a tight yellow bodycon dress and heels on—to meet him at Jack's.

No sooner had I introduced Taz and Nathan than he said he was going to go find his friends.

"I'll catch up with you later," he said, before rushing off into the crowd. I tried to dance off my disappointment, but I just wanted to leave. On the way out, I walked by Nathan as he danced with other girls. He pretended not to see me.

The next morning, I woke to a message apologizing.

Hey, I'm really sorry about last night. I hadn't seen my boy in a while. What are you up to tonight? I'll meet you wherever you are.

I'll be at Cobra. What time should we meet? I texted back. He didn't respond—not that afternoon, or as the evening went on. I dragged my feet at Cobra, checking my phone every few minutes for his message. We left early again. As we walked home, I saw his black-and-red plaid shirt. Just a few blocks away, Nathan was sitting right in front of Jim Bob's with his friend, flirting with two white girls.

I stood there, unnoticed. I wanted to cause a scene, say "What's Good?" then pop off in typical *Love & Hip Hop* style. But I composed myself, inching closer and closer as they continued to flirt, until I was standing right in front of Nathan. He only looked up when I said his name. He and his friend sat there looking like two busted-ass burglars. The girls immediately knew what was going on.

Nathan and I engaged in small talk before I wished him a good night and walked off, going home to cry melodramatically.

I spent all of Sunday waiting for an explanation while knocking back six Bud Light Limes and a whole pack of cigarettes.

I was angry that I didn't speak up the first night he arrived, that I had continued to give him chances. Was he intentionally trying to hurt me? Did he care about me at all? I was mad. Angela-Bassett-in-*Waiting-to-Exhale* mad. I wanted to channel her as Bernadine when she finds out her husband is leaving her for a white woman. I wanted to shout "A WHITE WOMAN IS THE ONLY ONE WHO COULD TOLERATE YOUR SMUG ASS!" and then put his shit on the curb and burn it. I imagined being Robin, schooling her no-good man Troy from the balcony as she breaks up with him for being trifling, dodging the oranges he throws in humiliating defeat. I thought about storing my anger until we met for drinks before hitting Nathan with Savannah's epic line to Kenneth, where she claims she's not mad, "And to prove it, the drinks are on you," before dumping my rum and coke over his disproportionately big head.

Instead, when he messaged me on Monday apologizing again, I ignored it.

As final exams wrapped up in April and Taz and I figured out whether we'd spend our summer in London or go back to Toronto, I finally accepted Nathan's apology. He begged me to stay in London so he could visit for a few weeks. "I need you," he said. And because movies had taught me that impulsive decisions are romantic, I stayed behind.

What I forgot about movies is that boys lie.

During that month and a half in London, Nathan and I only texted a handful of times—even then, he didn't seem interested. Taz had gone home so Nathan and I could have the house to ourselves, but now I was alone. I had stayed here on a whim for a guy who had burned me several times. Why did I think anything would be different this time around?

Worse—why did I think I deserved to be with someone who wasn't sure about me? That revelation was enough for me to be done with him. I deleted his number, and called Taz, who was more than happy to come back and spend the rest of her summer in London.

The night she returned, we went for a drink at Jack's. The bar was nearly empty.

"I'm so tired of being treated like shit," I said to her, hunched over the counter. "I'm ready to actually fall in love."

As I took a sip of my beer, a draft came through the entrance door, and in walked Amir.

Even under dim lighting, his smooth, dark mahogany skin, tinged pink at the tip of his nose, was radiant, and his jet black facial hair and straight white teeth were striking. He was no taller than me, but the way he carried himself—a sort of cool confidence without arrogance—made him seem much bigger than he was.

He was wearing a black-and-white sweatshirt and a black New York Yankees baseball cap. His eyes, deep brown, almond-shaped, and shrouded by dark circles, were already on mine.

We started dating that night.

///

Amir and I spent the rest of the summer riding around London in his gold Honda Accord, sitting in "No Parking" spots drinking Tim Hortons double-doubles and smoking Belmonts while getting to know each other. During the school year, he went to university in Windsor but he came home on weekends to work to support himself, his parents, and his siblings.

During those summer days, he fixed cars with his uncle; and in the evenings, he worked at Cineplex. At all times, he was helping people in his Sudanese community: his Bluetooth earpiece was firmly secured to one ear and his phone was always ringing. He held it in his left hand; the right was reserved for smoking a cigarette, or animated gestures that accompanied his rapid Arabic.

He was notorious around London for driving with his gas tank sign flashing yellow and a trunk full of items that he'd find at Goodwill and resell. His serious, worried demeanour could be broken by his childlike laugh. Even when he was in a rush, he always made time to put on his watch and his bracelets, spritzing himself with cologne.

When I was around Amir, it felt like my heart was bursting out of my chest. When I found old traumas and behaviours from my relationship with Joshua resurfacing, he patiently helped me through it. When I wanted to quit, when I yelled—my primary defence mechanism—he spoke to me calmly. When I was out of control with fear and anxiety and I pushed him away, he gave me room to breathe. He promised he would never hurt me and that he would always be my friend, even if our relationship ended. I knew he was telling the truth.

I introduced Amir to my mother, and the two quickly became friends. When she'd visit, we'd all sit in her car, the two of them in the front smoking cigarette after cigarette, talking for hours. When my mom and I would argue, he was the only one who could calm us both down and get us back on track. I talked to him about my dreams of being a journalist, and though he didn't understand much about the industry, he pushed me to keep writing.

We shared the experience of being Black in London, and it brought us closer. I watched the way strangers engaged with him, the look on their faces when we were out in public, heard the questions ("Is this actually your car?" "Do you speak English?" "Where are you originally from?")—things I was also dealing with. We debriefed about our experiences during the day, shared old stories about discrimination and racism, and cheered each other up when we felt like we were drowning.

But, even before the end of that summer, Amir and I realized that we had fundamentally different values and beliefs, ones we both spent a lot of time explaining and defending. I was an opinionated twenty-year-old feminist, agnostic, and curious about experiencing everything. He was twenty-three and too serious, following cultural and religious expectations with haphazard dedication. Amir came from a strict Muslim family; as the oldest son, he felt he had to set an example for his younger siblings, and that meant working hard, focusing in school, and not dating, especially outside of his religion and community. The Sudanese community in London is small and tight-knit; so, while I had already introduced him to my mom, he wasn't ready for people to know about me.

We drove around the city with tinted windows—"For your privacy," he'd say. He'd drop me off to get my groceries and wait in the car. If he forgot something at his house, he'd park the car in the communal lot and run in, me sitting alone with the radio on, watching the late-evening sun fall into darkness. He never stayed the night at my place; instead, he'd drive home bleary-eyed in the early morning before his parents woke up.

When school started again in the fall, Amir went back to Windsor to begin fourth year while I stayed in London and went into third. Every other weekend, I'd take the Greyhound to see him. We'd study together in the campus library—finally able to be together, away from prying eyes. He seemed much happier. But the pressures of emotionally and financially supporting his family made him detached and anxious. He decided to come back to London on some weekends to start driving his father's cab, a way to get fast money. He drove all day and night, and stopped by my place in the evening for an hour break, the only time I saw him. He'd sit on my couch, a distance away from me, on YouTube or texting, so into his phone that he didn't even hear when I spoke to him. Other times he vented—about money, about the stress he felt, about supporting his family. "You'll never understand. You were born here," he'd say. "I've been through real shit you'll never experience."

Every time he didn't hear what I said because he was on his phone, every time I put my hand on his or moved closer without reciprocation, I quietly nursed the rejection. I weighed the risks of asking for what I needed. When I finally brought it up, suggesting we try to spend more time together without distractions, that it would make me feel appreciated if he returned my affection, he said I was being dramatic, crazy, and irrational, that women shouldn't behave like this—they should learn that men are busy, and just suck it up. He didn't have time for my complaining, not when I didn't understand real struggle. "This is my life and you know this," he said. "I won't stop you if you want to leave."

I didn't want to leave, I just wanted to stop feeling invisible. Amir made it seem like I was asking for too much. I had done the opposite of what the magazines said. I was not cool and chill and compliant, and now I was being told by the guy I loved that I was being needy and delusional. I'd offer him the easy way out: if he was so overwhelmed with his priorities and I was adding more stress to his life, we could end it. Then he would put that responsibility back on me, a resolution never in sight.

It was hard to talk to Taz about my relationship. It felt like she wasn't there for me. She hated being single, so she spent more time dating, cancelling our girls' nights in, our weekend plans, and skipping her week to clean the house. She would boast about all the things she could do with her dates that I confided that Amir wouldn't do with me—ride around in the car with windows down, go on trips during the weekend, spend time together in public. With Amir in Windsor and Taz never home, I focused more on school and writing. Taz started going out with some girls she met at her part-time job, and when I'd be leaving to pull an all-nighter at the library, she and her friends were pre-drinking in the living room in their little black dresses and stilettos, asking me to come with them. When I got back home, empty bags of chips and red Solo cups were littered across the table, along with spilled vodka. Upstairs, Taz was asleep in her own bed, still in her sequined dress.

I was gravitating towards the people in my Women's Studies courses and had recently joined our campus V-Day group, an organization with chapters around the world, started by playwright and activist Eve Ensler to help fight violence against women and girls. We put on plays and helped organize the London SlutWalk and Take Back the Night. I loved being among women who were fierce advocates for sex positivity, who could recite any feminist text and engage in conversations about social issues that I cared about. I felt challenged by the discussions we were having—a well-needed departure from rehashing party stories with Taz. Still, I felt guilty that I enjoyed their company more than my best friend's.

Over the years, Taz and I shared so much with each other about our lives and who we were, but we never spoke about who we wanted to be, as if to admit that wanting something larger than the life we knew together was a betrayal of us. But I'd needed more from our friendship as I navigated the trauma of assault. I'd needed more when I became a target of race-motivated attacks when we went out at night. And now, I needed my friend to support my choices.

My interactions with Taz, once full of giggles, now consisted of tight-lipped smiles and desperate attempts to pretend everything was fine. She looked down or away from me when we spoke. Her body tensed beside mine. Our interactions felt hostile. Eventually, when I left for the library, Taz's friends stopped saying hello altogether, a silence filling the room. When I went to the mall now, I walked past the greeting card store. Neither of us wanted to address what was happening.

One evening in late fall, I was getting dressed to meet my new friends for dinner, but I couldn't find the blouse I wanted to wear. I had just bought it, the tag was still on. I asked Taz if she had seen it, and she offered to help me look, but it didn't turn up. As the weeks went by, more of my clothes started to go missing. When I opened the kitchen pantry or freezer to cook, my food was gone. Letters from collection agencies piled up in the mailbox, jammed in to make room for new ones. While I studied in my room, I could hear the unknown-caller ringtone chime loudly from Taz's phone, left unanswered. And then our internet and cable got disconnected, despite the monthly payments I gave her.

One weekend when she was out with her friends, I went down to the basement to do my laundry. I found a handful of my clothes in her basket, including my now-worn blouse. In a suitcase she kept downstairs, I found the remainder of my missing items, some stained and ripped from careless wear.

Taz and I had grown up together, seen each other through awful fashion trends and coloured contacts, high school crushes and overbearing parents. We had taken a chance on pursuing this adventure together, at the expense of our relationships, comfort, security, and cultures. And the oneness—that closeness—that had gotten us through the first two years at Western made it hard to admit that it was not impermeable, that we could still grow apart. Taz faced different pressures at home—marriage, education, a career in health care—that didn't disappear even as she got the freedom in London she desired. I was privileged to have very few family expectations. I had been raised to go my own way, to be my own person, to date who I wanted and at my own pace. She was raised to live life for her parents. She hated that she couldn't escape it; she hated that I could.

My friendship with Taz had been a bubble of safety and comfort. When we moved to London, we had only been focused on having a good time, but I felt myself growing into someone new—a woman who cared about what was going on in the world, who needed more out of her university experience than just foggy memories.

I wasn't the perfect friend; I had inadvertently shoved my own freedom in Taz's face. I'd asked her to take this journey with me to Western with little regard for the very real limitations she would face when she went back home after graduation. Living away from home was a stepping stone for me towards further independence. But for Taz, each time we went to bed after a wild night out, every semester that flew by, came with the dread that these moments had an end date. By pushing her to disregard this, I had trivialized her reality.

By the end of February, in third year, the greeting cards that we once sent each other to get through tough times had stopped coming. Weeks before that, Taz had gone back to sleeping in her own bed. No one needed to say that we had finally reached the end of our friendship. And we never did, not even as I packed up my belongings and moved out of our shared home.

Leaving our beautiful, baby blue house was a bittersweet moment. Taz and I had found our house together. It was where we had built some of the greatest memories of our lives. When we had a bad day, when our hearts were broken, when we bombed a test, it was where we convened to comfort each other. It was where we learned to take care of our home and ourselves; a refuge after school; a place where we looked forward to seeing each other every day. Friends and lovers all came and left, but inside our house we always had each other.

My new place had no lavender-painted walls, no stairs to run down to greet guests, no porch to drink and sunbathe on, no hardwood flooring that made it easy to clean up spilled vodka or pasta sauce. The Victorian charm of the blue house—present in the creaking floors and old-style door knobs—was replaced by modern fixings. Home was now a spacious, carpeted, one-bedroom apartment with beige walls.

After classes ended in April, Amir returned to London to drive his father's cab full-time. I was taking summer courses before beginning my fourth year. While Amir worked, I studied and wrote stories—fiction, personal essays, screenplays. I'd roam around the city to kill time, sitting on park benches eating frozen yogurt or writing on my laptop at Starbucks. In the evenings, Amir stopped by on his break and I'd cook for both of us. I massaged his aching back and shoulders. I left him a key to my apartment so he could come in to eat and relax when he was done work, long after I'd fallen asleep.

I was still mourning the end of my friendship with Taz. There were no more movie nights, no more making dinner together, no more popcorn and venting—Amir didn't have time to do any of those things, and he didn't want to make the time, either. And I didn't even have Malcolm anymore. We'd stayed close after second year, but he had transferred to another school abroad. I planned dinners and nights out with the few friends who were still in the city, but Amir objected. Women didn't feel the need to do those things when they had a partner, he said. What would his friends think, knowing that his girlfriend was out without him, slutting around? He refused to discuss why it was okay for him to go out with his friends to clubs all night; his only answer was that there were just things men could do that women shouldn't.

I felt like a housewife, providing Amir with emotional and domestic labour, feeding him, listening to his problems, internalizing my own because he ranked his suffering as higher priority, sacrificing my social life—all because he felt it was a woman's job to care for her partner at the expense of herself.

I didn't feel fulfilled by this arrangement, but telling him started hours-long fights that always ended the same way.

"This is who I am. But I love you enough to let you go if you're unhappy."

"Maybe we're just too different," I'd say. But the next day, he'd call me as if nothing had happened. We fought every night after his late-night taxi shift, coming to the same conclusion: we loved each other too much to let go, but that was no match for the mountain of difference ahead of us. I had tried to find ways of changing who I was to make our relationship work. But I was slowly realizing that there was nothing wrong with me in the first place.

I was starting to feel myself bloom. This change felt physiological, like every atom in my body was bursting, like I was shedding my old skin and glowing with consciousness. Amir was wrong that exploring my values and beliefs—my adventurousness, my curiosity, my independence, my disregard for gender roles—made me hedonistic, abnormal, and unladylike. And I had let his judgement shame me into thinking I was a bad, immoral person.

I was still working through what it meant to be in a relationship—what I owed Amir as my partner, and what he had no right to ask for. His expectation that I change in order to fit into his life was starting to feel like a deal-breaker. After so many years of changing who I was to fit into other people's lives, to make myself convenient and small, I was finally giving myself permission to walk away from people who didn't nurture my growth. For once, I felt fiercely protective of myself. This meant I no longer wanted to explain myself for the sake of someone else's insecurities, or be less of myself to make others feel comfortable.

A month before my fourth year was over, Amir asked me if I wanted to get engaged. I thought he was joking.

"Don't you want to get married soon? It's the next step," he said.

"I don't think that's our next step right now. We've got a lot of things to figure out," I replied.

"I'm going to ask your mom's permission anyway," he said, with a grin.

I knew my mother would never tell Amir what he wanted to hear. Too many times over the course of our relationship, she had pointed out that her daughter was not meant to sit at home and put her life on hold for a man. They had spent many moments together, sitting and smoking in each other's cars, talking about me. They spoke on the phone sometimes, she was like a second mother to him. They were honest with each other about everything—my mother sided with me when she thought I was right, and she told Amir and me when we were both acting foolish. And he was being foolish now, asking a woman he knew he wasn't compatible with to spend the rest of her life trying to fit into the mould of what he wanted. "You're a good person," my mother said when he called her about the engagement. "But you're not right for my daughter."

A couple of weeks later, he asked me again about marriage. I asked him a question back: if we got married, what did that mean for my way of life—hanging out with friends, socializing, going out? Unacceptable for a married woman, he said. My mouth? Too opinionated. My writing? Too explicit. My freedom? We'd be living with his parents—people I still hadn't met—and they'd make the rules.

I looked at his face—he seemed almost excited, like he thought I was considering his proposal. I realized he didn't know me at all—worse, he thought who I was as a person was a phase, that I'd be willing and able to change my politics, my pastimes, my stubbornness, my independence, my unruly, unladylike behaviour, my nasty, filthy mouth—all for a ring. I wanted love, to be loved, to feel love for someone else, and I wanted it so badly that I'd attached myself to someone whose acceptance was conditional on toning myself down silently and dutifully.

As a teenager, I had completely lost myself in my relationship with Joshua, whose control over me had made me afraid of getting stuck with the wrong guy. Now in my early twenties, I was in another relationship, which was controlling in different ways. Amir was a gentle guy, he was a *nice* guy. He wasn't the man you ever had to worry about stepping out on you. And that kind of reassurance alone would be enough for some women to jump into the matrimonial pool and hope the issues resolved themselves. I knew I had found someone who wouldn't abandon me like my father. But the mere thought of settling for this life made my stomach twist and my breath shorten. I wanted to be that woman for him. I wished I could provide the kind of submission he needed, hoping I'd like it, that it would be something that I wanted to do. I wondered what was wrong with me, why I couldn't just bow down, why the thought of settling and living with a half-hearted decision made me erupt into a cold sweat.

Perhaps it was because I had seen what settling could do in a marriage. Some of the women in my family had done it: played their domestic roles, raised kids (and grandkids), behaved modestly and conservatively. I saw them stay at home, cooking, cleaning, and caring for their children and elderly parents and in-laws while their husbands earned the money—and if they also worked, they still had to perform the same amount of emotional and domestic labour at home. They didn't have a choice, as a woman of their generation, to abandon the expectations of their family, culture, and religion. Some of them broke their silence: *If I had known. If I could do it over again. If I was a young woman during your time. If I was a woman like you.* I had seen the torn, pained look on their faces, their own fear of just how far their regret ran.

My mother has never cared for marriage. As the only person in the family without a spouse, she doesn't let the judgement of others bother her. She is unapologetically herself: loud, opinionated, independent. She refuses to change for anyone. My own grandfather, the only one among his siblings to marry for love, put aside the beliefs he was raised with to make sure that my mother didn't settle for my father, and to make sure that I never needed to rely on a man to take care of me. He raised me as a daughter, but with the leniency of a grandparent, and he encouraged me to live a full life without apology. He pushed for me to get an education, to be smart, to think for myself—to know myself before even *thinking* of marriage. He has never criticized the way I've chosen to live my life, never called me unwomanly or unnatural for not following the status quo.

I wasn't raised to be what Amir wanted. We both had to accept that.

As the end of my four years at Western loomed, I fell out of love. And Amir knew it too. I would be starting my Master of Journalism program at Ryerson in Toronto in the fall, and I needed to focus on this new chapter in my life. I didn't want to argue about going out with new friends or worry about whether my decisions—the ones that I made in my best interests—would offend him. I didn't want to put myself second anymore.

After final exams finished in April, I moved back home. Amir and I spoke every couple of days, though there was nothing to talk about. In June, I went back to London for my convocation; Amir brought me flowers, and sat with my family, proudly taking photos. A week later I took a three-week trip to Europe. The day before I left, I texted him. *I'll talk to you when I'm back.*

Okay. Have a safe flight, he responded.

When I landed back home, I messaged him, but he didn't text back. Not the next day either, or the rest of the week. I tried to keep busy as I prepared to move into my new place in Toronto before the start of my Master's, but I couldn't stop thinking about the deafening silence coming from Amir. One evening, my mother and I talked about Amir as we sat in her car. I slumped into the seat, hurt and angry. "He could've at least had the decency to tell me it was over," I finally said.

"He called me a few days after you came back," my mom said, putting a cigarette between her lips and lighting it. That day, they were on the phone for hours, talking about their own regrets, and about our dying relationship. "You were right," Amir had told her. He had made the mistake of trying to change me, but we were just too different. "I love her, so much," he said. "But I have to let her go."

Long before Amir, I had been searching for stability. He wanted to provide that, but on his terms. In the nearly two years we were together, he'd wanted me to be better, to be responsible for my life and what I wanted for myself. With his patience, I learned that I could cope with my emotions instead of numbing them with alcohol and partying. He showed me how to communicate in conflict. He pushed me towards a career in writing and supported me emotionally as I applied to grad school. He helped me spend more time with family. He encouraged me to be confident in who I was becoming as a woman.

Yet Amir saw my beliefs and values, my own personality, as needing refinement. He saw my needs—for him to accept me as I was, to be there for me, to match the effort that I put in—as irrational and selfish. He wanted to be a good partner—and in many ways he was—but our definitions of what made a relationship work differed. And because he had qualities that I needed in a partner that the other men in my life had lacked, I chose my own silence in order to be the perfect person, to live with the discomfort of not having my basic needs and expectations met so I could continue to access and hold dear the good parts of our relationship. Just like I had done with Joshua and Nathan, and even Taz.

Just like I had done with my father.

///

I would be lying if I said that I've become better at relationships since graduating university. One of the hardest things I've had to come to terms with is how I've silenced and policed myself, all in the hopes of being that cool girl who gets the guy, gets the best friend, gets the coveted life.

My desperation to be the model child for my dad, to behave perfectly, to not communicate my disappointment when he didn't show up, deeply impacted my romantic relationships: I moved through them with the same kind of inaction and made the same kind of excuses. I shrugged when men let me down. I let them take advantage of my patience and love. I hoped that if I said nothing but gave everything maybe they'd see I was the perfect woman, the model woman, that they'd stay. When I did finally find my voice, I was shoved into silence again by accusations that I was hysterical, crazy, irrational, selfish. I've chosen partners who were crooks, scrubs, abusers, liars; people who are physically and emotionally absent. I've given many chances before leaving. When I finally do walk away, I have nothing left of myself.

Harder still is understanding that this path did not start with the men I loved, but the man who made me. From conception, my father has played an insignificant role in my upbringing, and yet those fleeting moments with him have had a lasting impact on who and how I love, including how I love myself. I still greatly fear abandonment and rejection. I still worry any flaw will turn someone off, and they'll leave me waiting on the doorstep like my father did, never to be heard from again.

It's difficult to understand how these small moments have embedded themselves so deeply, when my grandfather—my only source of male stability and security—has ensured I never feel abandoned or unloved. He did more than my father ever could, more than a grandfather ever needs to. But this is the unfortunate evolutionary, psychological, and biological reality of the father-daughter relationship: they can be long gone, or they may have never been there to begin with, yet we still feel that ghost pain, that dull ache, that haunts us.

I'm still learning what I need from relationships, and each year I get better at finding what that is. I know that requires using my voice. I know that means putting myself first. I now know that there is nothing attractive about not having needs and expectations. Having needs does not make you unlovable. Wanting care, love, and support is not weak, needy, or selfish. It is not sustainable to live on scraps to feed the needs of someone else. Over the years, I've walked away from people I loved, who took everything but gave nothing, who only cared about me when it was beneficial for them. But advocating for what I need—loving myself—is greater than settling for love that is conditional.

It's still a challenge to speak up when Chill Girl is waiting to jump out of my throat and downplay my concerns to avoid abandonment. It's even more difficult to walk away—far away—when my needs aren't being fulfilled. But that doesn't mean that my independent ass doesn't want and deserve to be loved.

Because we all do, friends. We need love. The real kind of love that is complete and whole—no almosts or maybes. The kind that makes you a priority, not a late-night text. The kind that is communicative and fair, that doesn't hurt you or make you feel that you have to hide who you are. Love that isn't ashamed of you. Love that chooses you and appreciates you as a person and a partner. Love that doesn't delegitimize and dismiss your feelings, that doesn't call you crazy and emotional. Love that respects your needs and respects you. Love that accepts love and wants to give love back.

I want this for all of you. I want this for myself. I'll let you know when I find it.

The Token in Public

WHAT TO EXPECT: You will need to dodge Permit Pattys, BBQ Beckys, Pool Patrol Paulas, and all the other watch-persons who are just trying to be nice, do-gooding citizens by calling the police on you. While running errands, strangers will strike up a conversation and ask where you're from. They'll guess *Africa* (they haven't figured out yet that it's not a country). Oh, you're not? Maybe Ethiopia then, like those children in World Vision commercials.

A random person may approach you to tell you about a Black childhood friend or a former lover, who they will describe in great detail as if there's a chance you'll know them. People will also remember your face: That Black girl who went to Metro and bought a whole cake for herself. That Black girl who catches the 5:10 p.m. bus. That Black girl who once picked her dress out of her ass when she thought no one was looking.

HOW TO DEAL WITH IT: Capture all POCs (persons of caucasity) using the phone they think you can't afford to publicly shame them. White lies will help you get through the questions people will ask about your hair, clothing, background, and "accent." Also, just pick your wedgie, eat your damn sheet cake, and take your public transit at your designated time—recognition is inevitable.

at
all
costs

"Have you seen that Black girl? The one with the curly hair? She's so hot."

The limo driver went on and on about her to Amir as they leaned on their cabs, waiting in the queue by the London Music Hall for customers. He often saw her around the city and wanted to talk to her, he told Amir, but he was always driving his cab, and she was always in a rush. So he'd slow his limo down to a creeping roll behind her, studying her body, watching her hips swing when she walked.

He knew some things about her too. She was a student at Western. On weekends, she walked down Talbot Street to get to the Greyhound station, carrying her PINK roller bag. She lived somewhere near Oxford and Richmond, because in the evenings she carried grocery bags from the nearby Valu-mart. Once, he followed her and her friend down the road as they walked to Jack's, their legs wobbling in their cheap stilettos. That day he parked his cab at the entrance and went inside. He found her, touched her arm, and said hello. She looked confused by this smiling random older man in a suit, his bald head glistening with beads of sweat—it was so hot that night—but she smiled anyway, a smile that made the hairs on his arm stand up and his dick hard.

The translation from Sudanese to English only captured a fragment of its intent: "If you gave me five minutes with that girl, man, I'd fuck her so hard I'd give her back her pussy in her hand."

The translation of how sorry he was—that he didn't know, that he wouldn't have said it if he had known she was Amir's girlfriend—was about the same.

I had occasionally seen a limo slow down, but the tinted windows made it hard to see who was driving. I had once seen the whites of his teeth and the flick of his hand as he waved. It had never occurred to me that I was being followed.

Amir told the limo driver to never look my way again, or he would let all the other drivers know what kind of man he was. I never saw him after that.

I was comforted by Amir's threat, and I knew the guy would take it seriously. After all, his limo was his livelihood. His reputation and his income hinged on his acceptance among the rest of the drivers in London. How easy it was to stop following girls around so that none of the other men thought badly of him. How easy it was to go from wanting to fuck a girl so brutally that he ripped her apart to apologizing not because he had disrespected her but because he had disrespected her boyfriend. And yet how difficult it was for me to understand that, as a woman, the most dangerous things aren't as obvious as we've been trained to see.

///

The wet grass sloshing underneath my shoes from another rainy spring day was the only sound I heard as I walked through the field and back to my residence from the gym. The sky was a gloomy blue, the sliver of dawn illuminating the vastness of the field. As

I approached the middle of the field, a pile of flowers and a few bouquets were lying on the grass, colourful and startling against the greyish landscape.

Had someone died here? There were no cards, photos, or candles. Back at residence, I read through the *Western Gazette*, but nothing was mentioned.

The next day, I cut through the field again. Bright and piled high against the vast quietness were even more flowers—striking violets, soft pinks and deep yellows. Some had been pulled from nearby trees.

I still couldn't find answers in the paper to explain the swelling scene. Yet whispers made the rounds about a female student who had been sexually assaulted in the field. Some claimed they were friends of the survivor; others said they'd heard it from the survivor herself.

Gossip or not, the school's silence around the possible crime was too loud to ignore. Women were scared; we wanted an update, to squash the rumour if it wasn't true, so we could get on with our days, to cut through the fields like before, to walk back home after a late night at the library. The possibility that a rape had occurred on campus destroyed the assumption that we were entitled to protection in this communal setting. And we expected justice—for that woman and for ourselves, who knew just how easy it was to be raped, beaten, or killed while walking alone at night, while heading to the gym before dawn to get a workout in before class, while taking a run around the campus. We expected that, if there had in fact been an assault on a student, the school where we chose to study and live would acknowledge it. For many of the women on campus, including myself, it was like being silenced once again.

I went back to the gym later that week. The flowers, along with whatever horrors happened there, had been swept up and tossed away. The grass continued to grow and athletes carried on, their cleats ripping up the earth—and along with it, its secrets.

/ / /

Our first-year dorm floor was co-ed, and not co-ed at all. There were about thirty of us. One side housed all the guys, and down the middle of the hall were the remnants of a frame, possibly a former divider or door. On the other side was the girls' hall. Taz and I lived right at the crossing. We spent our evenings constantly passing through, in the boys' rooms and back to our side. By the end of the first month, the novelty of seeing people walking down the hall in their bath towels wore off. When the men's bathroom was flooded, which was often, it was normal to see them in ours, walking out of the bathroom in their flip-flops with their shower caddies, or brushing their teeth surrounded by our makeup and hair products on the countertops. We became more like family, and we made a pact: no one would commit dormcest—no hooking up. No relationships meant no drama.

There are many secrets in dorm rooms—ghosts of past inhabitants' regret and darkness etched into walls behind the blu-tack that holds up our posters, or seeped into mattresses that we cover with fresh sheets. Broken friendships, sadness, lacklustre experiences, true horrors. I thought about what those walls contained. I wanted as fresh a start as I could get; a clean slate from the girls before us. I wanted to make new memories—wild memories—to look back on years later, and to think of our tiny room as ours. But I did. I had to, when the room ended up housing some of my deepest secrets.

Of the secrets that people did talk about, one of the best-known was about the older male sophs, our student life mentors.

They exited from these rooms in the middle of the night, begging the first-year girl they treated as a little sister to not say a word, her promise collecting among the other promises in the walls. Some male sophs had favourites. He'd sit in the common room with her and her awestruck friends, admired like a god. He'd lie on her bed doing his readings while she sat at her desk doing her own. He'd come to our dorm parties and never leave her side, drinking with the younger frosh when he could be out in the city at a club with his legal friends. Some of us found it odd, inappropriate even. "We're just friends," they'd both assert, giggling.

The stories were similar. One routine movie night turned into something different. One night the door closed and he changed. One night he was aggressive, pinning her to the bed. If a girl refused, she was stonewalled and made to feel guilty for leading him on, until she gave in. Some girls wanted to stop but he wouldn't. One girl was covered in bruises, one had a bite mark. In the fall, one girl with shining eyes sat with him and her friends in the cafeteria; by winter she was alone and red-eyed.

The girls I knew were afraid to speak up. They didn't want him to lose his job. They didn't want to be blamed—people saw them flirting, they'd think she was lying. They didn't want him to retaliate, not when there were three more years to go. They blamed themselves for welcoming it, for not doing enough to stop it, for being in a place between their bodies screaming "no" and their will collapsing in.

It took me several years to come to terms with what happened between Joshua and me in my own dorm room. People weren't yet talking as openly about sexual assault and consent in 2010 and the proliferation of stories from women sharing their experiences wouldn't arrive for several more years. This was just before the shift in how we started talking about sexual assault—before the Steubenville case, before Jian Ghomeshi, before Brock Turner, before #IBelieveSurvivors, #MeToo, and #TimesUp. Before journalists really started digging into sexual assault in institutions across Canada and before the next generation of brave young women stormed their college and university campuses demanding accountability and justice.

And even though the outcry against sexual assault on campuses has become too loud to ignore, we still talk about campus sexual assault as something that is perpetrated by strangers—at parties and while walking home alone at night—but nearly 90 per cent of women who are raped in university and college are raped by someone they know. I was raped on campus during a party, not by another student or stranger, but by a boyfriend who didn't attend the school. So, where did I fit into the narrative, if at all?

Even though I learned more about consent from various campaigns on campus, I still didn't know that you could be raped by a boyfriend, that you could also enjoy intimacy with the same person who forced it on you. I also didn't know that consent cannot be given by someone who is under the influence of drugs and alcohol. I don't know if Joshua knew any of this either, but I can't give him the benefit of the doubt. He was a master of trickery, pushing my boundaries, equating love with sexual obligation. He knew how to wear me down until I surrendered, then treated my defeat as desire.

I didn't tell anyone about any of it, unsure if I could handle the questions: *If he was always forcing you to have sex, why did you do it? Why did you give in? If he was removing condoms, why didn't you do more to prevent yourself from getting pregnant? That night, why did you drink so much? Why didn't you talk to him about it? Why did you stay with him, then? Why do you women call everything rape? Why don't you women take some accountability for putting yourself in that position?*

The word *why* is inherently filled with blame and accusation.

Why asked me what choices I had made that caused my boyfriend to look bad. *Why* didn't ask him about his choice to do bad things. *Why* demands that survivors answer for being assaulted. *Why* doesn't demand that abusers be held accountable. Who needs the term *victim-blaming* when we have *why*?

Why did you go to his place? Why did you wear that dress? Why didn't you tell the police? Why didn't you speak up sooner? Why do you think it's okay to ruin his life? Why do you think this happened to you?

Why? Why? Why? Why? Why?

Why don't you fucking ask him?

///

Rape culture, a term coined in the U.S. in the 1970s, is, at its core, the way that society blames women for sexual assault while normalizing sexual violence. It is the promotion of violence against women—in films, TV, and ads. It is the belief that sexual assault is an inevitable part of life: women get raped, and men rape.

There is no larger hub of rape culture than university and college campuses. In 2014, 41 per cent of all sexual assaults in Canada were reported by students, and 90 per cent of those victims were women. In 2017, following the #MeToo movement, police-reported sexual assault (including on school grounds) hit a record number not seen since 1998. Women under twenty-five experience the highest rates of sexual violence in the country—before and after #MeToo.

Sexual assault is the most-reported crime on campuses—one in five women will experience some form of sexual assault while in college or university, and the first six to eight weeks of school are called the "red zone," the period when female students are most likely to be sexually assaulted. Fraternity members are the main culprits—numerous studies show that men who join frats are three times more likely to commit rape than their non-Greek counterparts, and that women in sororities are significantly more likely to experience rape than other female students. Just last October, the University of British Columbia shut down its fraternities and asked the RCMP to start an investigation after several girls said they were drugged at frat parties during a weekend.

Pro-rape messages begin from the first day of university, and aren't new. In 2013, Saint Mary's University in Halifax made news after hundreds of frosh were filmed chanting: "SMU boys, we like them young. Y is for your sister, O is for oh so tight, U is for underage, N is for no consent, G is for grab that ass." The chant had been a part of frosh week since 2009. The student president and vice-president resigned, and some of the student leaders were required to take sensitivity training. That same year at the University of British Columbia, first-year students on a school bus were reportedly encouraged to sing a similar chant. Student leaders quit and had to take part in sexual violence workshops.

In September 2016, Université du Québec students took part in a game that awarded points for completing a list of sexual challenges, such as taking a photo of a woman's breasts and kissing a woman. Reports suggested the student leaders could face expulsion, though no updates have been given to the public. And that same week at my own alma mater, students wrote "No means yes . . . and yes means anal" on the window of an off-campus student home. Following public outrage, and Western's silence, Glenn Matthews, the school's housing mediation officer, told the *London Free Press*, "I get it: the message is really bad, but students do dumb things." Western made headlines again in October 2019, when London's mayor Ed Holder called out students at Western's annual fake Homecoming party for promoting rape culture after banners were hanging outside off-campus housing that read "Queens

Girls Spit, Western Girls Swallow," "If Your Girl Goes to Western, She's Not Your Girl Anymore" and "Our Roommate Is a Virgin Pls Help," among others. While Western's president Alan Shepard, addressed the banners in a statement, calling it "casual misogyny," the letter didn't mention what the school would be doing about the students involved.

Dismissing or minimizing pro-rape messages as mere stupidity or poor behaviour is the same sentiment behind the "boys will be boys" excuse that fuels rape culture. Because rape culture is always about justifying the "unintentional" actions of boys and protecting them at all costs. And it's learned early on: in the wake of #MeToo, a camp of women, particularly mothers of sons, started using the hashtag #ProtectOurBoys to denounce what they believe is a culture of false sexual assault accusations by young women. That the lives of boys and men must be protected from the lies of girls and women who seek to destroy them.

Rape culture permeates every institution, from law enforcement to education to media, and it always upholds the futures of boys and men while blaming girls and women for the crimes committed against their bodies. When young women get raped, we question their intentions: *Are they sure they were raped? Were they drinking? How many men have they slept with? Are they sure they want to ruin a young man's life?*

Thanks to "Unfounded," the ground-breaking 2017 investigation by journalist Robyn Doolittle and the *Globe and Mail* investigative team, we know that, on average, Canadian police dismiss one in five reports of sexual assault. The *Globe*'s investigation not only brought to light the ways in which rape culture permeates law enforcement, but how it affects campus reporting.

The London Police Services had one of the highest unfounded rates in Canada, dismissing about 30 per cent of all sexual assault allegations between 2010 and 2014, the years I started and graduated from Western. Since the investigation, London's police chief John Pare has issued an apology to sexual assault survivors who had a negative experience with London police, and promised that his force will review unfounded cases as far back as 2010.

And if students are going to the police to report a sexual assault only for it to be considered baseless, universities don't offer much better support. Considering the prevalence of incidents, the data on reported sexual assaults on Canadian campuses is shockingly sparse. And post-secondary policies on sexual assault only contribute to re-victimizing and silencing survivors. In March 2016, following harrowing stories and an outcry from students and advocates around the province, the Ontario government passed Bill 132, which made it mandatory for each college and university in the province to have a policy for dealing with sexual violence, as well as to collect information on reported rapes. This change came over two years after an investigation revealed that only nine out of seventy-eight Canadian universities had a policy in place. Bill 132 seemed like a promising start in dealing with sexual assault on campus and providing more support for students. However, the bill allows each school the flexibility to include (and exclude) what they want in their policy, and to choose how they will apply it.

A national, student-led action plan against sexual assault called OurTurn found that nine Canadian universities have policies that restrict survivors from speaking about their sexual assault. These gag orders also determine who survivors can talk about their assault with, and on what platforms. Some schools don't let the survivor know if the offender has been sanctioned. Eight schools had a section that discouraged "frivolous claims."

Frivolous. As if women are too hysterical, too untrustworthy, to recognize violence against their own bodies. The underlying question remains: *Are you sure you want to ruin this man's life?*

Ruining the lives of boys and men has been a key theme in high-profile sexual assault cases over the years. In Steubenville, Ohio, in 2013, teenage star football players Trent Mays and Ma'lik Richmond were found guilty in juvenile court of raping a sixteen-year-old girl. The survivor faced ridicule from both students and parents, who blamed her for being drunk and causing her own rape. Poppy Harlow, a CNN correspondent, said that she found the verdict difficult to watch because the two boys "had such promising futures, [were] star football players, very good students," and that she "literally watched as they believed their lives fell apart."

Rehtaeh Parsons was a Nova Scotian teen who took her own life in April 2013 after four boys gang-raped her, took a photograph of the incident, and spread it around her school. Two weeks later, supporters of those boys put up posters around Halifax, including in the area where Parsons's mother lived, that read: "Speak the truth. There's two sides to every story. Listen before you judge. The truth will come out. Stay strong. Support the boys." A week later, *National Post* columnist Christie Blatchford wrote a despicable op-ed claiming there was no proof that the fifteen-year-old was too drunk to consent to sex. The newspaper has since removed it.

In 2014, it felt as though the way we spoke about survivors and sexual assault in Canada shifted, when CBC Radio broadcaster Jian Ghomeshi was charged with four counts of sexual assault and one count of overcoming resistance by choking (he was later acquitted). Women in media, and colleagues of Ghomeshi, came forward to admit that his name floated around their whisper networks of men to watch out for. But four years later, the *New York Review of Books* published an essay by Ghomeshi on how his life had been ruined by the allegations, in which he called himself the "poster boy" for bad male behaviour. Following public outcry and the departure of Ian Buruma, the editor responsible for the piece, the *New York Review* wrote a lengthy editor's note admitting they didn't know all the facts of the case and the essay was only shown to one male editor before publication.

In 2015, Brock Turner, the nineteen-year-old Stanford University student who was convicted of three counts of felony sexual assault against twenty-two-year-old Chanel Miller, was only given six months in prison (he served just three) by Judge Aaron Persky. Persky cited Turner's father as a positive character reference—a man who argued that his son's life was ruined for "twenty minutes of action"—as well as the role alcohol played. "A prison sentence would have a severe impact on him," Persky said in his ruling. "I think he will not be a danger to others." Then came the mainstream #MeToo movement in 2017, which demanded we start believing women and pierce the bubble of protection around abusive men.

Of course, there is much to say about which boys and men we protect—white boys end up getting away with a slap on the wrist or a warning. Men of colour, already demonized by the stereotypes that work against them, are more likely to be arrested or jailed. And what does that say about women of colour, who are so rarely believed, who do not fit the image of the perfect rape victim? Though Black, Indigenous, transgender, and queer women, as well as women with disabilities, face disproportionately higher rates of violence, the overwhelming majority of women who report abuse are white and heterosexual. And like all women who don't fit into the myth of the ideal victim, there's also the fear of not being believed.

When did we start guilting women into being flattered by the unsolicited catcalls, the violence-tinged remarks about our bodies and what they'd do to us if they got us alone, the grimy, sweaty hands that grab and claw at our waists even as our bodies and voices say no? Why is it our responsibility to make a loud scene to have our decision respected? Who told men that a yes can't become a no, and a no is always a yes? Who promised men that they were entitled to women's bodies? And, most of all, why are women always held responsible for making sure they aren't raped?

These are the questions that women ask themselves—when walking home, when in a club or at a house party, when in the home of a man. This is the mindset that women must have when we are targeted, harassed, beaten, humiliated, raped, stalked, and killed, every single day.

When an entire generation of young women has been in this situation or knows someone who has—and, even worse, has been blamed for what happened—that is rape culture. When we blame young women instead of holding abusers accountable— when we blame the victim—that is rape culture. When people believe that women who come forward with their story of sexual assault ruin the lives and careers of men, that is rape culture. When we make products for women—consent condoms, rape whistles, wristbands that detect spiked drinks, underwear with a lock—instead of investing in education to teach boys not to rape, that is rape culture. When one in three women will be sexually assaulted in their lifetime, but we focus on the 2 to 8 per cent of false accusations (research shows the percentage is largely inflated because of improper or inconsistent protocols) to prove that women are liars, that is rape culture. When those who are sexually assaulted must wear the emotional and physical scars that their attacker has inflicted, and then are re-traumatized by a society that picks apart their credibility, that is rape culture.

We let abusive men get away with violence against women because society has enabled it. These men believe they're entitled to women, and turn to violation when that entitlement is met with rejection. So they rape us, hit us, ridicule us, shoot us, stab us, kill us—for not acknowledging their whistle or a "hey baby." For refusing to give out our number, for not smiling. For saying no. In the past few years, thousands of women have been killed or injured for saying no. *Girls* have been killed or injured by their classmates for saying no. These boys and men use aggression and intimidation to scare us, stalk and blackmail us, sending our intimate photos out for the world to see. They send threatening messages and texts to keep us in line. They try to loosen us up with spiked drinks and date-rape drugs so we're too helpless to say no when they pry our weakened knees apart. And if we do give in to sex, if we do consent to any of it, then we're bitches. Sluts. Whores. So, whose lives are actually ruined in the process?

Trying to speak out about rape culture, about violence against women, only begets more violence against women: doxing women for speaking up on social media. Sending death and rape threats to women and their children. Harassing their families. Stalking them. As we protect boys and men, they protect themselves behind the anonymity of the internet, in the space our excuses have created. And what we dare say to women is that they must have done something to deserve it.

This is rape culture, and this culture has created monsters.

We teach children that there is a world that lurks in the darkness under their beds at night—the gap between humanity and unspeakable horrors. We tell them it isn't real. But it exists. We live it every day.

///

The best part about our weekly V-Day meetings was seeing each other. We had a little nook in the lower level of the University Student Centre, a colourful room full of inspirational quotes by powerful feminists and queer activists, rainbow flags, anti-racist handouts, and information on sex, consent, and sexuality. We hung out there in between classes, or to enjoy a quiet place to study.

On one occasion, a group of us were waiting for our third-year Women and Violence course. This week's topic was sexual assault and the legal system. As we sat on the grey L-shaped couch, we talked about rape and reporting.

> *It's not easy to get your case to court.*
> *There are so many factors.*
> *I wouldn't even try.*
> *I did try—they didn't believe me.*

We all spoke about the complexity of being a woman and being believed; about the ways that sexual assault always seemed to be our fault. Then one of the women interrupted.

"Who here has been sexually assaulted?" she asked.

One by one, nearly every woman in the room raised her hand. I looked around, my heart racing as I contemplated raising my hand too. For so long, I felt that I didn't deserve to talk about it, that I should've known better, that I would be judged because it happened in the context of a relationship. I felt I didn't have the right to seek support in the aftermath, despite the assault sinking in and destroying my self-esteem and relationships for many years to come; despite it creating a legacy of self-destructive coping mechanisms I would later seek therapy for. But these brave women were also—some for the first time—speaking out despite their fear. I slowly lifted my arm, my fingers curling weakly into my palm, the last woman to raise her hand.

The women started to share their stories. It was a cousin, a guy she had just met, a soph, a friend, a stranger, a boyfriend. It happened in their beds, in their homes, in their dorms, at a party. It had been weeks, months, years. For some it went along with other forms of abuse. Many blamed themselves for not saying no, for being too drunk, for being in love. They commiserated about the black-and-white nature of sexual assault, the shades of grey they tried to make sense of. Many felt worried that the police wouldn't take them seriously, that the people around them wouldn't know how to react, that his life would be ruined if they told.

We cried for one another and for ourselves, for the ways we had all internalized this guilt, the way it had changed us, ripped away our trust and replaced it with terror and betrayal. It was a shame we carried with us, a heavy burden on the wrong backs, and yet there was no one able to help lighten the weight—until now. We told each other it wasn't our fault. And when the women had all finished speaking they looked at me, their eyes still wet. It was my turn.

It had been two years since I left my secret behind in my dorm room, a stain in the carpet for the next unsuspecting woman to walk on—negative energy that a first-year would try to clear away with the rest. But now it was no longer my secret, or my shame. Like the women in this circle, I had paid for the protection of my abuser, and the cost of that silence had ravaged my health, my sense of self, and my peace.

"I was raped in my dorm room by my boyfriend. But it didn't start then."

In this tiny concrete room of unspeakable tragedies, I had never felt more safe.

The Token Mall-Goer

WHAT TO EXPECT: Department Store Susan will follow you around, and so will her henchmen security guards. And if you don't buy something, you will do your damnedest not to look guilty when you exit. You will have an irrational fear that the alarm will go off from something you've worn 262 times already, and you will make sure you don't put your hands in your pockets for any reason, not even to answer that phone call from your mama. White employees will play uncensored versions of their favourite hip-hop songs when their manager's away, but will turn it off when they see you. The store clerk will immediately direct you to the excellent sales on the rack at the back of the store. Lucky you.

HOW TO DEAL WITH IT: Tell Sue that if she'd like a more satisfying career following you around as your personal assistant, you'd be happy to let her manager know. Learn your rights in case police or security try to pull some unlawful BS. Afraid of the alarm? Wait for someone else to walk out at the same time. Channel your inner Oprah— you will not let anyone take you to the rack of shame, even if that's all you can afford (nobody puts Baby in the back rack!).

the
end
of
the
rainbow

Fourth year had just begun when Zadie told me she was thinking of transferring out of Western.

"I just can't take it anymore," she said. Her body caved in like a deflated balloon.

Zadie was tired of all of it. The drunk white girls who followed her around bars asking to touch her hair; the white guys who harassed her and the men who wanted to "experience" her; the stares of curious people and the anti-Black slurs it seemed she heard more often than her own name. She dreaded the racially inappropriate comments from students who claimed they meant no harm, and the uncomfortable whiteness of her Ph.D. program. Her health was suffering too: she was so depressed and anxious about living in London and being a student at Western that she couldn't even get out of bed in the morning.

I told her to just hold on; it seemed more tragic to uproot herself in the final year of her degree. She had met some amazing people, women who were going through it with her—we would support her. Was it so bad that she couldn't wait a few more months?

Though I knew better than to defend staying here a minute longer, I didn't want to acknowledge that this place had the power, after everything we had already been through, to claim a Black woman's university career. But Zadie was gone before the end of the school year.

On numerous occasions, I had also considered leaving Western. I had weighed all the pros and cons: the hardships that I experienced on a daily basis and the new and possibly more challenging discomforts of switching schools. I had told myself that it wasn't that bad, even as tears of dread filled my eyes at the sound of my morning alarm. I tried all kinds of remedies to comfort myself—eating, drinking, watching movies, taking long baths, working out, writing—in the feeble hope that I'd find some interest and enjoyment in life again. Yet, like Zadie, I walked through campus hunched over in invisible pain, unsmiling and unhappy, in a constant daze of misery. I had made several great Black female friends over the past few years, whose presence helped me keep my sanity, but I missed Malcolm. Over text, he told me he was thriving at his new school. As a Black man in his new environment, he was feeling pretty good about his choice to leave Western.

Following the move out of the home that Taz and I shared, I threw myself into whatever I could: performing in and directing plays produced by V-Day, writing more on the weekends, and improving my grades so that I could graduate on time and apply to Master's programs.

Towards the end of third year, I walked by a flyer in the Women's Studies department advertising a new course called Black Women's History in Canada. It was the first time it was being offered in years—like many Afrocentric electives at the school, the department hadn't been able to fill the minimum seats needed to move it forward. This course was a deliberate and significant attempt to introduce more knowledge about Black women's history into the curriculum. I signed up, hoping it wouldn't get cancelled again, and waited for the class list to fill up.

On the first day, I walked into a room full of Black women and other women of colour. I looked at their faces—excited, nervous, relieved. They smiled at me as I took a seat. My muscles slowly untightened, my jaw unclenched. My sharp edges, the ones I carried as protection, that refused to let anyone get close, blurred into unfamiliar smoothness. A gentle yet rapid stream of emotion flowed through me: I was home.

The course was the meeting spot we had been desperately searching for. We laughed and cried and shook our heads and eye-rolled at stories of each other's experiences of racism, sexism, and student life. We bonded over our mutual exotification stories—the dreaded "I never _____ with a Black girl before"—and other Black-girl woes that plagued us while living in London: online dating, sexually racist pickup lines, nightlife, classroom politics.

We talked about ourselves, our relationships, our identities, our homelands. We were angry for one another and we cheered on each other's successes. Our experiences of objectification and exotification were alarmingly similar, as were our responses: rage, sadness, humiliation, distress, shame, depression, resilience. There was no one here to tell us we were exaggerating, that we were just bitter, that our anger and pain was unjustified. For three hours every Wednesday, we were finally able to put down the heavy burden that we had been carrying on our backs throughout the week; and just be in good company.

The consensus was that we weren't getting what we needed at Western—academically, emotionally, spiritually. The class was a quiet place to vent and a site of communal encouragement and commiseration. We were shoulders to weep on, bodyguards for one another, voices of reason, familiar faces on campus.

There is something life-changing about Black female friendship, especially during a dark time. We know pain, but we also know it won't last forever. We know the transformative power of joy and laughter, the strength of sisterhood, the support of a good "mhmm" or an empathetic head nod. We know that Black female friendship can keep you alive, that sisterhood is essential to survival. But sisterhood is not just about building an unbreakable support system of boss bitches; it's possibly the only space where Black women are allowed to safely be the opposite—soft, emotional, vulnerable. It's also a space to celebrate our successes and triumphs, and to admit that the burden of acting the part of the unbreakable Black woman is crushing us.

"Black Girl Magic" is a term that was popularized in 2013 by CaShawn Thompson to celebrate all the dopeness, beauty and strength, that encompasses Black women and womanhood. Yet however glorious Black Girl Magic may be, it can trap us—once again labelling Black women as superhuman and impervious to pain. Black Girl Magic should be about celebrating our resilience— but also about admitting when things aren't right. Sisterhood gives us a place to talk about both.

We also need sisterhood because our collective reality is, at times, grim. Some research shows that Black women are the most likely group to be unarmed when killed by police. We are more likely than white women to experience sexual assault and intimate partner violence. Black trans women face disproportionate rates of violence and homicide. Black mothers are more likely to die in childbirth.

While Black women are leading or founding social justice movements around the world—from #MeToo to Black Lives Matter—that also uplift white women and Black men, Black women rarely get the same support for our causes in return. This is why sisterhood is essential for Black women's survival: irrespective of physical or digital space, it's a place for Black women, for once, to be for and about ourselves.

Others depend on our anger to move their causes forward, yet when we are angry for ourselves, our anger is unjustified. So often, Black women's anger is weaponized against us. From TV and film tropes to politics, the legacy of the Angry Black Woman has trivialized Black women's rage, painting our expression of pain as aggressive, hostile, unwomanly—or worse, as comic relief. While being an angry or emotional woman is trivialized as hysteria, for Black women it's dangerous.

Black women have to hold it all together for everyone else *and* ourselves—an expectation based on the historic misconception that we can handle taxing physical and emotional labour. Yet if the weight becomes too much, if we try to seek out emotional support like therapy, we're weak. If we talk about it publicly, we're entitled. Unlike our white female counterparts, being righteously angry can cost us our jobs and relationships, and possibly our lives. And unlike white women, our tears get us nowhere. Despite systemic and institutional oppression and discrimination, Black women are never allowed the chance to feel our anger, even when it stems from pain and sadness, even when working through it can be transformative and healing.

The past few years have been marked by women's rage, stemming from the #MeToo movement, which was started by Tarana Burke, a Black civil rights activist who used the term almost a decade before actor Alyssa Milano. Women are standing up against a patriarchal system that reinforces that women are inferior, deserving of being violated, left out, paid less, pushed out. But who is afforded rage? Who are the voices on the front lines who are praised and uplifted, and whose voices are still on the margins, scolded and shamed for also wanting their moment to be angry?

Black women's expressions of rage have been stifled for more than a century, from the first-wave feminist movement that cast aside the work of Black women for a mainstream white women's campaign. They secured property and voting rights for themselves while Black women were banned from demonstrations or forced to walk behind white women. Even today, Black women who speak up to share their #MeToo stories have been met with silence and skepticism from white female survivors (Black women have been sexual assault activists for centuries). Stories about police violence and anti-Black racism against female-identified people don't get the same kind of virality or outrage as their male counterparts, sparking the hashtag #SayHerName. We use our rage to push forward the causes of everyone else—uplifting other women, standing up for the rights of Black men—but in return, who's angry for us?

Society calls Black women bitter for expressing rage over social, political, economic, reproductive, and gender discrimination, but celebrates white women's rage as iconic and inspiring. Where white men are entitled to their rage—which is still considered non-threatening, even as it has caused some of the worst tragedies in North America in the past few years—Black women are punished for thinking they have a right to it. So we internalize it, leaving that rage with nowhere to go but darting around inside us until our health and well-being are destroyed in the chaos.

Internalizing rage can be detrimental, but vocalizing it can be transformative. Women's collective rage is both a healing and a political tool, and it's one that's brought attention to the actions of powerful men like Brett Kavanaugh, Harvey Weinstein, Bill Cosby, and Jeffrey Epstein. It's birthed new movements and protests: Black Lives Matter, the Women's March, SlutWalk. For

Black women, coming together with other Black women and voicing that rage can change the world.

Professor Brittney C. Cooper talks about this at length in her book *Eloquent Rage: A Black Feminist Discovers Her Superpower.* She details how institutions, from law enforcement to churches to the family unit to the White House, have played a role in limiting Black women politically, sexually, and economically, and how that has caused us good reason to feel angry. She encourages Black women to strategically express their anger and rage over their own oppression in order to make a change. Most of all, Cooper says, when Black women express their rage—their superpower—it benefits everyone.

The use of anger and rage as transformative for Black women is not a new concept. In 1981, Black feminist Audre Lorde gave a keynote address called "Uses of Anger: Women Responding to Racism" at the National Women's Studies Association conference. She said that any discussion among women about racism must include the recognition and use of anger as a tool, because our anger is an appropriate response to hatred. Unlike hatred, which intends to harm or disenfranchise marginalized people, the anger of Black women and women of colour is grief—an accumulation of injustice. Knowledge and power is within our anger, and it can be used as a collective, creative tool to change the world—and help each of us heal:

> Women of Color in America have grown up within a symphony of anguish at being silenced, at being unchosen, at knowing that when we survive, it is in spite of a whole world out there that takes for granted our lack of humanness, that hates our very existence, outside of its service. And I say "symphony" rather than "cacophony" because we have had to learn to orchestrate those furies

so that they do not tear us apart. We have had to learn to move through them and use them for strength and force and insight within our daily lives.

There are so few outlets for Black women to express this rage, making friendship and sisterhood essential. In these groups, we can be angry without judgement, without shame. We can talk about the shit that beats us down today and know that thanks to our friends, we can get through tomorrow. In our collective anger, we learn about each other and ourselves; we find the tools to fight oppression, to start healing from the inside and then start healing the world. Anger and rage are indeed our superpowers—but so are vulnerability and love.

/ / /

In my fourth year, I was performing in Eve Ensler's most successful play, *The Vagina Monologues*, spending my evenings rehearsing and hanging out with other people who were also involved.

I loved that group, as well as V-Day, but I was the only Black woman. And while Ensler's plays and campaigns have garnered global attention, Ensler has been accused of a reductionist version of feminism that doesn't understand or include the experiences of women of colour and trans women. I sought something more for the people who didn't see themselves represented in the plays on campus.

Inspired by the conversations we were having in my Black women's history class, I set out to include a new performance in our lineup, outside of the usual Ensler plays—something written by a Black woman that spoke to the power of sisterhood: *for colored girls who have considered suicide / when the rainbow is enuf*, by the late Ntozake Shange.

for colored girls, arguably Shange's most acclaimed work, is a choreopoem that was first performed in 1976. It follows the interconnected coming-of-age stories of seven Black women, named after different colours of the rainbow, who are navigating various aspects of life and love in an oppressive, racist, and sexist society, and how sisterhood uplifts and supports them.

I was drawn in by the relevance of the play—how nearly forty years later it was just as applicable to the conversations we were having in and outside the classroom. It felt symbolic to put the play on at Western: the last time it was performed at the school was in the early 1990s, and a professor who had been around then told me the roles were played by white women.

I placed call-outs for auditions across campus, and women of various faiths, gender identities, and ethnicities auditioned for roles. Some came from other schools. In the end, I cast a group of talented young women—women I knew, and others who had been looking for a play on campus for Black women.

for colored girls was challenging to choreograph. We were often stumped as to how to put each piece together. The play is a mix of poetry, spoken word, and song. We had difficulty with the rhythm and we struggled with the lyricism. We faltered when it required dancing. We stumbled over the punctuation and spelling. We spent nearly every evening rehearsing for hours on end, stopping only to eat and study. Some nights, we got little done, instead trading war stories about our time at Western. As opening night approached, we were nowhere near ready.

Each woman brought her own experiences to her character, and it was so poignant and heavy that we were often overcome with emotion. When the pieces started coming together, we ebbed and flowed alongside each other, as if each of us were made for our character, as if we were meant to find each other. School, as always, was rough. We were tired, stressed, and moody, but the one constant source of light was inside our rehearsal room in the dark basement of the Student Centre.

We had taken on the play to provide a space for women of colour to see themselves represented on campus, hoping they would feel relief from the alienation of being a woman and student of colour at Western. We'd had no idea just how bad we needed it ourselves.

/ / /

Not long after Zadie's confession, Jasmine told me she was also considering transferring to another school. I cast her as the Lady in Yellow in our play, and over rehearsals I learned that her reasons were similar to Zadie's: as an artist, the racism and microaggressions she experienced on campus and in the city had zapped her creativity. She had stopped going out to bars with her girlfriends—she was tired of being pointed out, laughed at, and harassed. Her friends thought she was exaggerating, and she was done trying to explain herself to dismissive ears. She was mentally and physically exhausted.

Then came Angela, only in her second year and ready to pack up. London—and Western—had broken her spirit.

Towards the end of my time at Western, more and more of my Black girlfriends were transferring out of the school, or at least considering it. Their stories became increasingly horrific—dummies lynched in trees, professors and students making racist comments in class, verbal attacks in the city—as did the physical and emotional toll. The symptoms of sadness, depression, anxiety, fear, and hopelessness were endemic in this environment. My friends were afraid for their safety, paralyzed by the thought that this was their reality for the next few years.

I would be graduating soon, and starting my Master's in the fall. One of the reasons I decided to go back home for grad school was that I wanted to be back in a diverse city. But, somehow, leaving Western for grad school felt like a betrayal. London had been my home for the past four years. I'd experienced a genuine kindness in strangers that I had never felt back home. It was both a protective cocoon while I blossomed into adulthood and a place that had been detrimental to my identity, to my health, and to the people around me.

I had the time of my life in London—I had more fun than I could've imagined. It may have not been how I expected it to go, but it was damn close. Coming here wasn't just about fun, textbooks, and passing grades—it was a test to see if I could handle life's unpredictability, if I could bend but not break, if I could be hardened but still soft.

///

The deafening roar from the crowd was too loud to be true.

I nervously peered out from backstage and was left speechless. Nearly one hundred seats were filled, and there were dozens of students and locals chatting and grabbing a drink at the bar, waiting for the show to start. It was the most Black women and women of colour I had ever seen in a space at Western.

Our second and final performance of *for colored girls* was taking place at The Spoke, an on-campus bar that doubles as an event space on the top floor of the Student Centre. Opening night, at a different venue, had been a flop. Only twenty people showed up and most were white; our nerves had gotten the best of us, and we forgot our lines. Moments we thought would be well received by the audience were met with deafening silence. We were all disappointed, and I considered cancelling our other performance. We had put so much of ourselves into this play. We had created a sisterhood. Wouldn't the audience see that?

For many of us, this play—the words in the book—were defining moments of our lives at Western. It was a refuge for the rest of our time here, and an extension of who we had become. And, like the characters in the book, we were connected to each other now; our colours formed a rainbow. Even in exhaustion and hopelessness, sisterhood does not give up on each other. We decided to move forward and do our last show.

Seeing all those women in the crowd—friends, strangers, elderly women, faculty, other students—we knew they also needed this play. We went on stage that evening and gave our last performance everything we had. We weren't just unnamed characters; we were nurtured by snaps and affirming hums and nods and laughter and applause. We gave back by being our truest selves, our most vulnerable, our bodies radiating love and grief and emotion.

The last four years had been lonely and hard, but also rewarding. Some days were so dull and grey it seemed like all the colour in the world had gone away forever. Some days, the sun escaped from the clouds and danced on our skin, and the beads of sweat that trickled down our temples reminded us that we were alive. We had carried on, through all of it, for ourselves and each other, under the darkened sky.

Towards the end of Shange's play, the women all come together onstage to recite a series of monologues called "no more love poems." The Lady in Yellow talks about feeling vulnerable as a Black woman and the belief that they are immune to emotional pain:

but bein alive & bein a woman & bein colored is a metaphysical
dilemma/ i havent conquered yet/ do you see the point
my spirit is too ancient to understand the separation of soul &
gender/ my love is too delicate to have thrown back on my face

At eighteen, I made the decision to come to Western, and I had experienced things I only thought were possible in movies. But it wasn't all about having a good time. I had enjoyed the tenderness of strangers as well as their rejection. I had felt the devastation of violence and loss and the healing of love and friendship. I had learned the power of my body—female, brown-skinned—to inspire both desire and hatred, to determine how I moved through the world. The experience was painful and healing, ugly and beautiful. And like the Lady in Yellow, I am still trying to understand the charged nature of my existence in this world—one that is highly politicized and racialized.

As Jasmine moved to the front of the stage to deliver the last line, the thickness of anticipation swelled between us. "And this is for colored girls who have considered suicide," her voice broke, "but are moving to the ends of their own rainbows." A sob ripped from her body, relief and pain at once. One by one, each of us onstage started to weep, a collective surge of emotion and exhaustion. In the audience, women wiped their own eyes and nodded in unison.

As we took our final bow to a standing ovation of teary-eyed audience members, I felt a lightness I hadn't known in years, a reassurance that everything was going to be okay.

Hand in hand, our full lips quivering and tears sparkling as they rolled down our melanin cheeks, we looked up as the grey sky burst open, showering us in warm, colourful light. The rainbow had been there all along.

epilogue

Less than two months after I graduated from Western, another Black teenager was shot and killed.

During a hot August day in Ferguson, Missouri, Darren Wilson, a white police officer, shot eighteen-year-old Michael Brown.

The case galvanized racial tensions in North America. Following a grand jury trial, Wilson was not indicted in the shooting of Brown.

Many people disagreed with Wilson's excessive use of force against the teen. Others believed Brown deserved to die. Social media was filled with racist posts, turning a video clip released by police into memes mocking Brown's life and death.

By now I was extremely familiar with the danger of such stereotypes, a consequence of living in a predominately white city: that Black bodies are seen as less receptive to pain, unrapeable, unbreakable, inherently criminal, violent, unruly in their shapes and colours, resistant to authority. That bodies like mine must be suppressed and silenced for being loud, for talking back, for knowing our rights, for not being respectable enough, for not being grateful enough, for not fitting in, for walking late at night, for driving, for breathing.

In the Western bubble—in London's bubble—I had been so focused on navigating my own life as a student that I didn't realize that the world around me was quickly changing. And this was, in part, a deliberate act of self-preservation. I couldn't be invested in making sense of the oppression surrounding me when I needed to find ways to protect myself from it. But as I dealt with my own world, we were already entering a highly polarized culture—made even more apparent by Brown's death—where people brazenly justified attacks on Black bodies for refusing to give in to the systems that oppress them, then tarnished their memories by reducing them to racial stereotypes.

Brown's death launched Black Lives Matter on a global scale. Protests burst from North America's seams—a collective anger over police practices that have for so long been excessive against bodies of colour. Tear gas, fire, and chants of "Hands up, don't shoot" and "No justice, no peace" defined the summer. The simmering pot of racial tensions had finally spilled over, bringing with it a rage and resistance so fierce that it blazed a path for a new era of civil rights in the twenty-first century.

I had once believed that what I'd experienced was a London problem, a Western University problem, a Southwestern Ontario problem. I naively believed that I could file away the last four years of my life and return to my ignorantly blissful self: a teen with no sense of the world, an overprotected child, a body untouched by violence and hate. But I returned home to a different place than I'd left, and it had only gotten worse. Diversity and multiculturalism were suddenly a hindrance to "Canadian values." Anti-Islam rhetoric saw more attacks on innocent Muslim people. Police violence was also reaching a boiling point, after the fatal shootings of two Black men, Jermaine Carby and Andrew Loku, and many other cases of excessive force against Black, brown, and Indigenous bodies.

White supremacists were holding rallies, crashed by anti-racist protesters; white pride flyers were strung across campuses;

alt-right media personalities were renting public space for events. And while there have been victories for those who fight for the humanity of everyone, the battle is still ongoing.

It's easy to conclude that hate has trickled in from Europe's wave of right-wing populism. Or, more directly, from south of the border, following the election of Donald Trump—a man who has admitted to sexually assaulting women, is trying to erase trans people from history, and throws immigrants and children in inhumane detention centres. However, Canada has its own long history to contend with. Under the guise of multiculturalism, we've conveniently forgotten Canada's own contributions to racism: colonialism and genocide against Indigenous communities; two hundred years of slavery; police and state violence against marginalized people; the removal of Black and Indigenous children from homes; the endless and continual cases of missing and murdered Indigenous women, girls, and Two Spirit people; a historic rise in hate crimes; the 2017 Quebec City mosque shooting and the 2018 Toronto van attack; far- and alt-right politicians in government; alt-right and white nationalist rallies that happen in cities around the country. In April 2019, the *Globe and Mail* revealed the thriving right-wing extremism in Canada after obtaining more than 150,000 private chat-room messages.

The Canadian Anti-Hate Network has long been tracking hate incidents, as have researchers like Dr. Barbara Perry, Dr. Ryan Scrivens, and Dr. David Hoffman, who have warned about the rise of far-right extremism in Canada for decades. Only now is our society, and our government, starting to pay attention.

At the same time, the resistance has never been stronger. Women are coming forward with their stories of sexual assault. LGBTQ2S+ people are still fighting for human rights and legal protections. Indigenous folks are demanding truth and reconciliation from our governments. Black people are holding law enforcement and the justice system accountable, and won't settle for less. The media is taking a greater interest in stories about racism and sexual assault, and digital spaces give underrepresented voices places to share their own stories. Perpetrators are *sometimes* being held accountable. The message is clear: the time to act is now.

This resistance is not just about marching down the street or staging a physical protest. It's in the health researchers collecting race-based data, the writers covering underreported stories, the lawyers representing clients against state violence, the experts documenting violence against women, the teachers pushing for more inclusive curriculums, the journalists and advocates risking their lives for the truth. It's in the tools we use in this fight against hate: social media to share our stories and engage with others; video to capture unlawful acts; retweets and shares that expose injustices and counter false information. In this new era, born out of past hard-won freedoms and causes, fuelled by rage and unity, we all can play a role in dismantling systems that have benefitted from keeping us silent.

When we look at our institutional spaces, few have been as revolutionary as universities and colleges. From the formation of historic Black colleges in the U.S. to Black student activism in the civil rights era to centuries of scientific breakthroughs, institutions of higher education have always been much more than a place to study (they also have an inescapable history: the slave economy built many colleges in the U.S.). While historically a site encouraging polarizing ideas, the battle between hate speech and free speech has become one of the cornerstones of university discussions.

Student life has also changed. It's no longer about juggling school, part-time jobs, and relationships; instead, students are fighting to feel safe and included on campus—tearing down alt-right flyers and counter-protesting far-right events, demanding schools remove statues of racist figures, fighting ineffective school policies on sexual assault, and hosting Black-only graduations to celebrate convocating in an education system that disproportionately expels and suspends Black students. Our young generation—the group so often misjudged and infantilized—is leading one of the greatest movements in the country against far-right extremism, racism, and sexual misconduct.

But there is a price to pay for standing up for what's right: harassment, doxing, loss of opportunities, threats, violence. There are whispered concerns from others, sometimes even our own families, to stay quiet, to not make a scene. There are dismissive comments: that we're exaggerating, crazy, too sensitive. Others firmly remind us to know our place—they tell us that we must respect authority, that we deserve harm if we don't.

I opened this book with a quote that is often attributed to author Zora Neale Hurston. "If you are silent about your pain, they'll kill you and say you enjoyed it."

It is not surprising that powerful institutions aim to silence the voices of the marginalized and twist their truths to benefit their own narrative. Neither is it surprising how stereotypes are reproduced and maintained to justify discrimination and violence against queer and trans people, and against bodies of colour. How misogyny turns us against women to maintain gender inequality. Those oppressed under systems of oppression are always at the expense of the oppressor's narrative. But the status quo knows the power our stories have to make these systems crumble.

But this death that Neale Hurston talks about is also metaphorical. If we don't speak up, our silence will kill every one of us. If we let ourselves be told our experiences don't matter— that we are too young, too old, too unworthy, too angry—we will internalize our pain and it will eat us alive. Sharing stories is an evolutionary action: oral storytelling has been practised around the world since ancient times, a way to pass on values, narratives, and culture to future generations.

Storytelling today often comes in the form of writing, putting pen to paper or fingers to a keyboard, a way to mark our permanent place in the public record. Writing in itself is radical resistance, a triumph—people can try to stop you from speaking your truth, but no one can take your words from you.

Personal writing by marginalized groups has often been treated as lazy and self-indulgent by the same critics who praise white male memoirists. Yet writing about oneself has long been a means of survival for the most marginalized groups: survivors of slavery, residential schools, neo-segregation, conversion therapy, and abuse. There's a reason these memoirs continue to be popular: they braid together our common threads of pain, trauma, joy, and healing. They remind us that, though much has changed for the better, some things have stayed the same. That all struggles and victories are tied to past history, and that history will repeat itself if we don't start to rewrite it. Our voices can join a legacy of stories that have changed the world, that create quiet revelations and roaring revolutions.

We did not put ourselves in this current cultural climate, but we *are* responsible for getting each other out. I have complete faith that we can: we are glowing with rage, the kind that can shatter glass ceilings and scorch the earth. We are emotional with grief, with tears that can flood oceans and put out blazing fires. We are soft with compassion, yet powerful enough to dissolve borders. Our words are cutting, deep enough to slash through the pages of history and write it anew.

So, write and live your truth. Speak up. Rage. Because the time for silence has passed.

acknowledgements

This book has been a ten-year journey with many people to thank.

Thank you, thank you, thank you from the depths of my heart to every single person who knew there was a book inside me or helped me along the way. Thanks for sharing your knowledge, for checking in on me, for encouraging me, or just listening to me panic, stress, or worry—sometimes for hours on end. You all reminded me about the end goal, and my own power to carry this book through.

Thank you to the editors who've helped shape some of the ideas in this book through past articles I've written. Josh Visser: thanks for letting me write about London for *Vice Canada* back in 2015—it turns out there was even more to say.

To my agent, Stephanie Sinclair: thanks for believing in this book and its concept as ferociously as I did. Your support and voice of reason means everything to me.

To my editor, Haley Cullingham: as a Black woman, I worried that I would lose the essence of this book in the editing process, and along with it, my voice; instead, you made my words shine even brighter. You brought nuance and depth to this book with such thoughtfulness, compassion, and sensitivity. Thank you for pushing me when I needed to be pushed, and making sure that I was putting out a book I was proud of.

To Jared Bland, and the M&S team: thank you so much for believing in me and the power of this book. Your enthusiasm, from the very beginning, made this whole process even more special.

Ally: thank you so much for making sure I put out the best version of this book—and on such short notice!

Davide: thanks for reading my cringy first draft and being kind enough to frame your feedback in a way that maintained our friendship. I'm glad you did cause this version is soooooo much better.

Carly Lewis: you sat with me at Aroma when I was a baby journalist and listened to me despair about whether I could fit into this industry and write this book—and you did everything you could to make me feel that I could do both. Thank you!

Alicia: you've been ride or die for me for so many years, and I can't ever thank you enough. Many parts of this book and earlier drafts were inspired by you and our conversations.

Dwayne: I couldn't have made it through without you. You kept me cackling and hopeful. I hear your voice every day, even though we are miles apart. Thanks for your Black Excellence, it's most certainly rubbed off on me.

Catherine: for 10 years, there hasn't been a single text message, card or conversation between us where you haven't told me how proud you are of me. You saw me when I couldn't see myself, and you kept me writing when I couldn't write anymore. I couldn't ask for a better friend. I love you.

Tanya, Tony, Chantelle, and Anahla: you became a part of my life as I was writing my story, then a part of this book. In the little time we've spent together, you've been incredibly supportive and encouraging, even through the parts that can hurt. Having you in my life drives me to do better every day. I hope I made you all proud.

Francesca: I met you late in the process, but you've saved the day more than once. Thanks for always being there for my biggest meltdowns, and for all the times you cured my writer's block just by taking me outside for air and letting me vent.

Arvin: thanks for being my light when things feel dark, and for helping me make tough and exciting decisions about this book. You keep me sane and smiling. Clowns forever.

Thanks to all the professors at Western and Ryerson who invested in me both inside and outside the classroom. Michael Arntfield: It was in your class that my kernel of an idea for this book came together, and you were the first person to believe that it could be something great. Lisa Taylor: Your diligence and care as my MRP advisor helped me form an integral part of this book.

Thanks to Barbara Perry, Gaye Warthe, and all the other experts who took the time to speak to me over the years for both this book and past articles that became a part of this project.

Thanks to all the scholars, theorists, activists, and writers who inspired my own writing and kept me afloat in my darkest times: bell hooks, Laura Mulvey, Audre Lorde, Sojourner Truth, Dionne Brand, Brittney C. Cooper, Patricia Hill Collins, Toni Morrison, Ntozake Shange, Sara Ahmed, Frantz Fanon, Roxane Gay, Gloria Anzaldúa, Judith Butler, Alicia Elliott, Kiese Laymon, Hélène Cixous, Kimberlé Crenshaw, Angela Davis, James Baldwin, Barbara Smith, the Combahee River Collective, Deborah Gray White, and so many more.

To my grandmother: you read to me every night and your love had no limits. You shaped my future, and even though we only had a few years together, they were the greatest a child could wish for. I miss you every single day.

To my mother: you drove from home to London in snow storms, sometimes just to surprise me with spoils from home.

You still do it when I'm sad, sick or while I was working on this book, which has felt like an eternity for you. That is a testament to your love. You've been my best friend and partner-in-crime. You are a force of a woman, and you've taught me how to harness my own winds.

To my grandfather: there are not enough words in the universe to describe how grateful I am for your love, support, and presence in my life. You've been a parent, a grandparent, a mentor and a role model. You've never once doubted me or my path. Then, just when I thought this book would be the one thing you wouldn't be able to support, you surprised me once again. You're the reason I was able to even go to university, so this book is just as much yours. It would take lifetimes for me to thank you; I hope this book can be a start. (Sorry it's not as PG as you'd like.)

And finally, thanks to everyone who shared their stories and fears and made it safe to share mine. To those who spoke to me about their harrowing (and beautiful) experiences in London, at Western, and in cities and universities around the country. It's not an easy thing to go through, nor an easy thing to talk about. This book is yours too.

about the author

ETERNITY MARTIS is an award-winning Toronto-based journalist. She was a 2017 National Magazine Awards finalist for Best New Writer and the 2018 winner of the Canadian Online Publishing Awards for Best Investigative Article. Her work has appeared in Vice, Huffington Post, *The Walrus*, CBC, Hazlitt, *The Fader*, Salon, and on academic syllabuses around the world. Her work on race and language has influenced media style guide changes across the country. She is the course developer and instructor of Reporting On Race: The Black Community in the Media at Ryerson University, the first of its kind in Canada, and the 2021 Journalist-in-Residence at the University of British Columbia. She earned an Honours Bachelor of Arts and a Certificate in Writing from Western University and a Masters of Journalism from Ryerson University She is also a winner of Canada's Top 100 Most Powerful Women by Women's Executive Network.

Her debut memoir, *They Said This Would Be Fun*, was a *Toronto Star*, *Globe and Mail*, and *Vancouver Sun* bestseller. It has been featured on anticipated and essential book lists including *NOW*, the *Globe and Mail*, BlogTO, CBC, *Chatelaine*, and more. CBC has named Martis one of "Six Canadian writers of Black heritage to watch in 2020" and the book as one of "20 moving Canadian memoirs to read right now." PopSugar named it one of "5 Books About Race on College Campuses Every Student

Should Read" and it was named a "Best Book of 2020" by Chapters/Indigo and Apple. The audiobook was named "Best Audiobooks Of 2020" by Audible. The book also became a finalist for the International Book Awards in the categories of Autobiography/Memoir and Social Change.